Puppet Reporting and Monitoring

Create insightful reports for your server infrastructure using Puppet

Michael Duffy

BIRMINGHAM - MUMBAI

Puppet Reporting and Monitoring

First published: June 2014

Production Reference: 1100614

Published by Packt Publishing Ltd.
Livery Place
35 Livery Street
Birmingham B3 2PB, UK.

ISBN 978-1-78398-142-7

www.packtpub.com

Cover Image by Gareth Howard Jones (garth123@hotmail.co.uk)

Credits

Author
Michael Duffy

Reviewers
Ugo Bellavance
Johan De Wit
James Fryman
Jason Slagle
Eric Stonfer

Commissioning Editor
Edward Gordon

Acquisition Editor
Llewellyn Rozario

Content Development Editor
Sankalp Pawar

Technical Editors
Taabish Khan
Aparna Kumar

Copy Editors
Insiya Morbiwala
Aditya Nair
Stuti Srivastava

Project Coordinator
Puja Shukla

Proofreaders
Maria Gould
Paul Hindle

Indexer
Mariammal Chettiyar

Production Coordinator
Sushma Redkar

Cover Work
Sushma Redkar

About the Author

Michael Duffy has been working in systems administration and automation for more years than he cares to remember, and is the founder of Stunt Hamster Ltd.; a small but perfectly formed consultancy that helps companies, both small and large, deliver fully automated and scalable infrastructure. He has consulted for companies such as O2 and BSkyB, delivering design, automation, and monitoring of infrastructure for products that serve millions of users.

Michael is a keen advocate of DevOps methodologies and is especially interested in using automation to not only deliver scalable and reliable systems, but also to make sure that people can see what is actually going on under the hood when using reporting tools. If given the chance, he will happily spend hours telling you how fantastic it is that people from the development and operations fields can finally talk and go to the pub together.

I would like to thank my absolutely incredible wife, Beth, and my fantastic daughter, Megan, for enduring more than their fair share of enthused lectures about Puppet reporting and for ensuring that I was fed, watered, and occasionally moved out into sunlight when I became a little too focused on writing. Without your love and support, this book wouldn't have been possible.

I would also like to thank the editors and staff at Packt Publishing; without them, this book would be several hundred pages of extreme gibberish without a gerund verb in sight.

About the Reviewers

Ugo Bellavance has done most of his studies in e-commerce. He started using Linux from RedHat 5.2, got Linux training from Savoir-faire Linux at age 20, and got his RHCE on RHEL 6 in 2011. He's been a consultant in the past, but he's now an employee for a provincial government agency for which he manages the IT infrastructure (servers, workstations, network, security, virtualization, SAN/NAS, and PBX). He's a big fan of open source software and its underlying philosophy. He has worked with Debian, Ubuntu, and SUSE, but what he knows best is RHEL-based distributions. He's known for his contributions to the MailScanner project (he has been a technical reviewer for *MailScanner User Guide and Training Manual, Julian Field* published by the University of Southampton, Department of Civil & Environmental Engineering), but he has also given time to different open source projects such as Mondo Rescue, OTRS, SpamAssassin, pfSense, and a few others. He's been a technical reviewer for *Centos 6 Linux Server Cookbook, Jonathan Hobson, Packt Publishing* and *Puppet 3 Beginner's Guide, John Arundel, Packt Publishing*.

I thank my lover, Lysanne, who accepted to allow me some free time slots for this review even with two dynamic children to take care of. The presence of these three human beings in my life is simply invaluable.

I must also thank my friend, Sébastien, whose generosity is only matched by his knowledge and kindness. I would never have reached this high in my career if it wasn't for him.

Johan De Wit was an early Linux user, and he still remembers those days when he built a 0.9x Linux kernel on his brand new 486 computer, which took a whole night. His love for Unix operating systems already existed before Linux was announced. It is not surprising that he started his career as a Unix system administrator.

Johan doesn't remember precisely when he started working with open source software, but since 2009, he has been working as an open source consultant at Open-Future, where he got the opportunity to work with Puppet. Puppet has now become his biggest interest, and he loves to teach Puppet as one of the few official Puppet trainers in Belgium.

Johan started the Belgian Puppet user group a year ago, where he tries to bring some Puppet users together by hosting great and interesting meet-ups. When he takes the time to write Puppet-related blogs, he does so mostly on `http://puppet-be.github.io/`, the BPUG website. From time to time, he tries to spread some hopefully wise Puppet words while presenting a talk at a Puppet camp somewhere in Europe.

Besides having fun at work, he spends a lot of his free time with his two lovely kids and his two Belgian draft horses, and if time and the weather permits, he likes to rebuild and drive his old-school chopper.

James Fryman is a technologist who has been working on spreading the good word of technology via the greatest mechanism known to man: the beer-fueled rant. He has been working to automate software and infrastructure for the last 10 years and has learned quite a bit about security, architecture, scaling, and development as a result. He currently works for GitHub as an Operations Hacker.

Jason Slagle is a 17-year veteran of systems and network administration. Having worked on everything from Linux systems to Cisco networks and SAN Storage, he is always looking for ways to make his work repeatable and automated. When he is not hacking a computer for work or pleasure, he enjoys running, cycling, and occasionally, geocaching.

Jason is currently employed by CNWR Inc., an IT and infrastructure consulting company in his home town of Toledo, Ohio. There, he supports several large customers in their quest to automate and improve their infrastructure and development operations.

Jason has also served as a technical reviewer for *Puppet 3 Beginner's Guide, John Arundel, Packt Publishing*.

I'd like to thank my wife, Heather, and my son, Jacob, for putting up with me while I worked on this and other projects. They make even days with critical systems outages better!

Eric Stonfer has spent the last 12 years working as a systems administrator with an emphasis on systems automation and configuration management.

www.PacktPub.com

Support files, eBooks, discount offers, and more

You might want to visit www.PacktPub.com for support files and downloads related to your book.

Did you know that Packt offers eBook versions of every book published, with PDF and ePub files available? You can upgrade to the eBook version at www.PacktPub.com and as a print book customer, you are entitled to a discount on the eBook copy. Get in touch with us at service@packtpub.com for more details.

At www.PacktPub.com, you can also read a collection of free technical articles, sign up for a range of free newsletters and receive exclusive discounts and offers on Packt books and eBooks.

http://PacktLib.PacktPub.com

Do you need instant solutions to your IT questions? PacktLib is Packt's online digital book library. Here, you can access, read and search across Packt's entire library of books.

Why subscribe?

- Fully searchable across every book published by Packt
- Copy and paste, print and bookmark content
- On demand and accessible via web browser

Free access for Packt account holders

If you have an account with Packt at www.PacktPub.com, you can use this to access PacktLib today and view nine entirely free books. Simply use your login credentials for immediate access.

Table of Contents

Preface

Puppet is possibly the fastest growing configuration management tool on the planet, and this is in no small part due to its combination of power and accessibility. From small five-node installations through to hugely complex cloud infrastructures that number thousands of nodes, Puppet has proven its ability to deliver on the promise of infrastructure as code. There have been a number of titles that cover its ability to create idempotent resources, manage services, and ensure that systems are configured correctly and maintained with little or no effort. Yet, none of these titles spend more than a chapter discussing its reporting features.

This is a shame; Puppet's reporting capability is one of its most overlooked yet powerful features. If used correctly, its built-in reporting abilities can give you stunning levels of detail about your infrastructure, from the amount of hardware used and networking details to details about how and when resources were changed. However, this is just the beginning. In this book, we are going to cover techniques that are simple to learn and that will allow you to use Puppet as a key part of your alerting systems, letting it bring your attention to important changes and even forming a simple-to-implement tripwire system. We're going to explore PuppetDB and learn why this is a fantastic source of information that you can use to not only explore the changes being applied to your systems, but also create an end-to-end repository of knowledge about your infrastructure. We're going to build custom dashboards to make this data accessible, and finally, we will look at the ways by which you can make Puppet not only report the changes, but also drive them.

What this book covers

Chapter 1, Setting Up Puppet for Reporting, will guide you through the simple steps to take your existing Puppet installation and make it report.

Chapter 2, Viewing Data in Dashboards, takes a look at the existing dashboards available for Puppet and how you can use them to report on your data.

Chapter 3, Introducing Report Processors, acquaints you with the engine that drives much of the Puppet reporting process—the report processor.

Chapter 4, Creating Your Own Report Processor, deals with creating your own report processor with custom e-mail alerts, MySQL storage, and integration with third-party products.

Chapter 5, Exploring PuppetDB, introduces PuppetDB, a fantastic and powerful system for report storage and analysis. In this chapter, we look at what PuppetDB is, how it's configured, and finally, how you can set it up in your own infrastructure.

Chapter 6, Retrieving Data with the PuppetDB API, explores the fantastically powerful API of PuppetDB; the API allows you to query your reports in a number of different ways. We're going to explore this API for functions that range from basic queries to advanced data integration.

Chapter 7, Writing Custom Reports with PuppetDB, deals with creating easy-to-use custom report applications.

Chapter 8, Creating Your Own Custom Dashboard, deals with creating an attractive and detailed custom dashboard using Dashing and PuppetDB.

Chapter 9, Looking Back and Looking Forward, takes a look at some of the more advanced ways in which you can use Puppet reporting to do everything from alerting to the orchestration of your infrastructure.

What you need for this book

The code and examples in this book have been designed for use with the following software:

- Puppet 3.0 and higher versions
- Ruby 1.9 and higher versions

Who this book is for

This book is designed for anyone who wants to learn more about the fundamental components of Puppet reporting. To get the most out of this book, you should already be familiar with Puppet and be comfortable with its major components such as the Puppet master and Puppet agent. You should also be comfortable with reading code, and in particular, you should be at least passingly familiar with Ruby. Finally, you should be happy working on the command line in the Linux/Unix flavor of your choice.

Conventions

In this book, you will find a number of styles of text that distinguish between different kinds of information. Here are some examples of these styles, and an explanation of their meaning.

Code words in text, database table names, folder names, filenames, file extensions, pathnames, dummy URLs, user input, and Twitter handles are shown as follows: "We can include other contexts through the use of the `include` directive."

A block of code is set as follows:

```
include puppet

Puppet::Reports::register_report(:myfirstreport) do
  desc "My very first report!"

  def process
    if self.status == 'failed'
      msg = "failed puppet run for #{self.host} #{self.status}
      File.open('./tmp/puppetpanic.txt', 'w') { | f |
        f.write(msg)}
    end
  end
end
```

When we wish to draw your attention to a particular part of a code block, the relevant lines or items are set in bold:

```
metric_vals = {}

        self.metrics.each { |metric, data|
          data.values.each { |val|
            name = "#{val[1]} #{metric}"
            value = val[2]
            metric_vals[name] = value
          }
        }
```

Any command-line input or output is written as follows:

```
puppet module generate <username>-<modulename>
```

New terms and **important words** are shown in bold. Words that you see on the screen, in menus or dialog boxes for example, appear in the text like this: "The **Facts** view is particularly useful as it not only lists each node with the associated fact value, but also presents it neatly in the form of a graph."

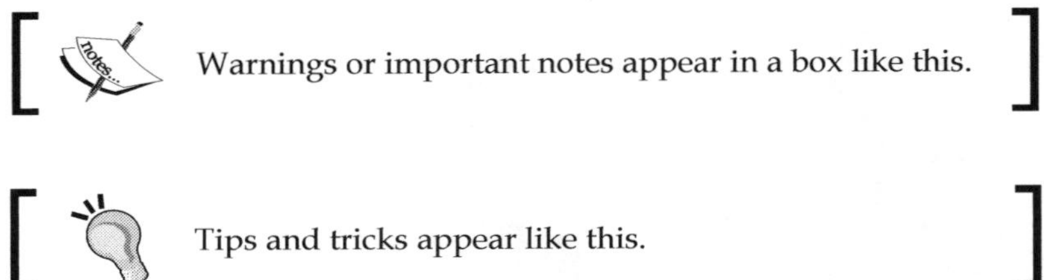

Warnings or important notes appear in a box like this.

Tips and tricks appear like this.

Reader feedback

Feedback from our readers is always welcome. Let us know what you think about this book—what you liked or may have disliked. Reader feedback is important for us to develop titles that you really get the most out of.

To send us general feedback, simply send an e-mail to `feedback@packtpub.com`, and mention the book title via the subject of your message.

If there is a topic that you have expertise in and you are interested in either writing or contributing to a book, see our author guide on `www.packtpub.com/authors`.

Customer support

Now that you are the proud owner of a Packt book, we have a number of things to help you to get the most from your purchase.

Downloading the example code

You can download the example code files for all Packt books you have purchased from your account at `http://www.packtpub.com`. If you purchased this book elsewhere, you can visit `http://www.packtpub.com/support` and register to have the files e-mailed directly to you.

Errata

Although we have taken every care to ensure the accuracy of our content, mistakes do happen. If you find a mistake in one of our books—maybe a mistake in the text or the code—we would be grateful if you would report this to us. By doing so, you can save other readers from frustration and help us improve subsequent versions of this book. If you find any errata, please report them by visiting `http://www.packtpub.com/submit-errata`, selecting your book, clicking on the **errata submission form** link, and entering the details of your errata. Once your errata are verified, your submission will be accepted and the errata will be uploaded on our website, or added to any list of existing errata, under the Errata section of that title. Any existing errata can be viewed by selecting your title from `http://www.packtpub.com/support`.

Piracy

Piracy of copyright material on the Internet is an ongoing problem across all media. At Packt, we take the protection of our copyright and licenses very seriously. If you come across any illegal copies of our works, in any form, on the Internet, please provide us with the location address or website name immediately so that we can pursue a remedy.

Please contact us at `copyright@packtpub.com` with a link to the suspected pirated material.

We appreciate your help in protecting our authors, and our ability to bring you valuable content.

Questions

You can contact us at `questions@packtpub.com` if you are having a problem with any aspect of the book, and we will do our best to address it.

1
Setting Up Puppet for Reporting

Some tools can be enormously tedious to set up for reporting, normally making you wade through many different configuration files, wrestle with obscure settings, and make you lose the will to live, generally. Fortunately, **Puppet** is a sensible product when it comes to its initial configuration; out of the box, it will take very little tweaking to get it to report to the Puppet master. This is not to say that there aren't plenty of options to keep power users happy, it's just that you generally do not need to use them.

In this chapter, we're going to cover the following topics:

- An introduction to how Puppet reporting works
- A brief tour of the Puppet `config` files
- Configuring a Puppet client
- Configuring a Puppet master

Learning the basics of Puppet reporting

Before we get into the nitty-gritty of configuring our Puppet installation, it's worth briefly going over the basics of how Puppet goes about its reporting. At its heart, a Puppet master is a web server and the reporting mechanism reflects this; a Puppet agent performs a simple HTTPS PUT operation to place the reporting information onto a Puppet master. When configured properly, the Puppet master will receive reports from Puppet agents, each and every time they perform a Puppet run, either in the noop or apply mode. Once the reports have been received, we can go ahead and do some fairly fantastic things with the data using a variety of methods to transform, transport, and integrate it with other systems.

The data that the Puppet agent reports back to the Puppet master is made up of two crucial elements: logs and metrics. The Puppet agent creates a full audit log of the events during each run, and when the reporting is enabled, this will be forwarded to the Puppet master. This allows you to see whether there were any issues during the run, and if so, what they were; or, it simply lets you examine what operations the Puppet agent performed if things went smoothly.

The metrics that the Puppet agent passes to the Puppet master are very granular and offer a fantastic insight into where Puppet is spending its time, be it fetching, processing, or applying changes. This can be very important if you are managing a large infrastructure with Puppet; a node that takes four minutes to complete isn't too bad when there are only a handful of them, but it can be downright painful when you are dealing with hundreds of them. It also allows you to start tracking the performance of your Puppet infrastructure over time. Puppet modules have a tendency to start as lean, but as they grow in complexity, they can become sluggish and bloated. Identifying speed issues early can help you refactor your modules into smaller and better performing pieces of code before they start to impact the overall stability and speed of your Puppet infrastructure.

The data derived from the logs and metrics build up a complete picture of your hosts and is enormously useful when it comes to diagnosing issues. For example, without reporting, you may have a hard time diagnosing why every single Puppet agent is suddenly throwing errors when applying the catalog; with reporting, it becomes a relatively easy matter to spot that someone has checked in a common module with a bug. Many sites use modules to manage DNS, NTP, and other common items, and a typo in one of these modules can very quickly ensure that every single host will report errors. Without reporting, you can make shrewd guesses as to the fault, but to actually prove it, you're going to have to log onto multiple nodes to examine the logs. You are going to end up spending a fair chunk of time going from node to node running the agent in the noop mode and comparing logs manually to ensure that it is indeed a common fault. This is based on the assumption that you notice the fault, of course; without the reporting in place, you may find that the nodes can be in poor shape for a substantial time before you realize that something is amiss or that you probably have not been running Puppet at all. Running Puppet on a host that has not been managed for some time may produce a list of changes that is uncomfortably long and could potentially introduce a breaking change somewhere along the line. There are many reasons why a Puppet agent may have stopped running, and you can be in for a shock if it's been a month or two since Puppet was last run on a host. A lot can change in that time, and it's entirely possible that one of the many non-applied changes might create problems in a running service.

Where the **Parser** is the brains of Puppet, the **Facter** is its eyes and ears. Before Puppet compiles a manifest, it first consults Facter to figure out a few key things. First and foremost, it needs to know where it is and what it is. These are facts that the Puppet agent can deduce by consulting Facter on elements such as the node's hostname, the number of CPUs, amount of RAM, and so on. Facter knows a surprising amount of information, out of the box, and its knowledge increases with each release. Before Facter 1.7, it was possible to use Ruby code, shipped as a Puppet plugin, to extend the facts you could gather. However, with Facter 1.7, you can also teach Facter some new tricks with external facts. External facts allow you to add to Facter's already prodigious knowledge by including anything from Ruby scripts to plain old YAML files to insert data. These additional points of data can be utilized within Puppet reports in the same way as any default Facter item, and they can also be used to add additional context around the existing data.

Now that we know the basics of how Puppet reporting works, it's time to go ahead and configure our Puppet master and agents to report. I'm going to make the assumption that you already have a working copy of either Puppet Open Source or Puppet Enterprise installed; if you haven't, there are some excellent guides available either online at `http://Puppetlabs.com/learn` or available for purchase elsewhere. If you're going to buy a book, I recommend *Puppet 3 Beginner's Guide, John Arundel, Packt Publishing*. It is an excellent and complete resource on how to install and use Puppet.

The example configurations I have used are from the latest version of Puppet Open Source (Version 3.2.2 and higher), packaged for Ubuntu. Your configuration may differ slightly if you're following this on another distribution, but it should broadly contain the same settings.

Exploring the Puppet configuration file

Let's take a look at the default configuration that ships with Puppet Open Source. By default, you can find the `config` file in the `/etc/puppet/puppet.conf` directory. The configuration file is as follows:

```
[main]
logdir=/var/log/puppet
vardir=/var/lib/puppet
ssldir=/var/lib/puppet/ssl
rundir=/var/run/puppet
factpath=$vardir/lib/facter
```

```
templatedir=$confdir/templates

[master]
# These are needed when the puppetmaster is run by passenger
# and can safely be removed if webrick is used.
ssl_client_header = SSL_CLIENT_S_DN
ssl_client_verify_header = SSL_CLIENT_VERIFY
```

The first interesting thing to note about this configuration file is that it can be used for the Puppet agent, Puppet master, and Puppet apply commands. Many items of the configuration file tend to be common items such as log directories, run directories, and so on, so there is no real need to keep a separate version of these files for each role. Again, this is an example of the common way that Puppet has been designed, when it comes to configuration.

The `puppet.conf` file is split up using the standard `ini` notation of using configuration blocks to separate roles and the common configuration. The most common blocks that you will encounter are `[main]`, `[agent]`, and `[master]`, although sites that have implemented either Puppet faces or Puppet environments may have more. Generally speaking, as these additional configuration blocks are not used to set up reporting, we shall ignore them for the purposes of this book.

The `[main]` configuration block is used for any configuration that is applied regardless of the mode that Puppet is run in. As you can see from the preceding configuration file, this includes locations of SSL certificates, logs, and other fundamental configuration items. These are generally things that you should keep the same on every host, regardless of it being a Puppet master or agent. However, it's worth noting that you can override the settings in a configuration block by setting them in a more specific block elsewhere in the file. Any setting in the `[main]` configuration block is available to be overridden by any subsequent block further down the configuration file.

The `[master]` block is used for all configuration items that are specific to the role of the Puppet master. As you can see in the default configuration file, this includes items for **Phusion Passenger** configurations, but more importantly for us, this is also where you would set items such as the report processor and its options. For our initial setup, we're going to use the master configuration to set where our reports will be stored and ensure that we are using the store report processor.

The `[agent]` configuration block is utilized when you run Puppet as an agent. It is here that we can set the fairly simple configuration required to make the Puppet agent communicate reports with the Puppet master. We won't be spending much time in this configuration block; the majority of the configuration and processing of the Puppet reports takes place on the Puppet master rather than on the client side. There are some exceptions to this rule; for instance, you may have to amend a client-side setting to make the Puppet agent report to a different Puppet master.

Alternatively, if you are using the HTTP report process, you may wish to set a different URL. So, it's worth having an understanding of the options that are available.

> **Why use a separate Puppet report server?**
>
> As with all good enterprise solutions, Puppet has been designed to allow certain roles to be decomposed into separate components to ease scaling. Reporting fits into this, and you may find that if you are using report processors that are resource intensive, then you may want to separate the reporting function onto a separate server and leave as many resources as possible for the Puppet master to deal with client requests.
>
> You can find a complete list of all configuration options for Puppet at `http://docs.puppetlabs.com/references/latest/configuration.html`, including the options for directing reports to a separate Puppet master.

Setting up the server

For the most part, the Puppet server is preconfigured for reporting and is simply waiting for clients to start sending information to it. By default, the Puppet master will use the store report processor, and this will simply store the data that is sent to the Puppet master in the YAML format on the filesystem.

> YAML is a data serialization format that is designed to be both machine and human readable. It's widely used and seems to have found considerable favor among open source projects. YAML has a simple layout but still has the ability to hold complex configurations that are easily accessible with relatively simple code. A nice side effect of its popularity is that it has gained first-class support in many languages and for those languages without such support, there are many libraries that allow you to easily work with them.
>
> It's worth taking some time to become familiar with YAML; you can find the YAML specifications at `http://yaml.org`, and Wikipedia has an excellent entry that can ease you into understanding how this simple yet exceedingly powerful format is used.

Although the store processor is simple, it gives us an excellent starting point to ensure that our Puppet master and agent are configured correctly. The YAML files it produces hold a complete record of the Puppet agent's interactions with the client. This record includes a complete record of which resources were applied, how long it took, what value they were earlier, and much more. In later chapters, we will fully explore the wealth of data that both the Puppet reports and Puppet metrics offer us.

> We're going to spend some time looking at various settings, both in this chapter and others. While you can look in the raw configuration files (and I highly encourage you to), you can also use the `puppet master -configprint` command to find out what Puppet believes a particular setting to be set at. This is extremely useful in finding out how a default setting may be configured, as it may not even be present in the configuration file but will still be applied!

Out of the box, the only real Puppet master setting that may require some care and attention is the `reportdir` setting. This defines where the Puppet agent reports are stored, and it is important that this points to a directory that has plenty of space. I've routinely seen installations of Puppet where the disk is consumed within a matter of days via a `reportdir` setting that points at a relatively diminutive partition. By default, the `reportdir` setting is set to the `/var/lib/puppet/reports` directory. So at the very least, make sure that your `/var` partition is fairly roomy. If your Puppet agents are set to run every thirty minutes and you have a healthy number of hosts, then whatever partition you have this directory in is going to become full very quickly. It's worth bearing in mind that there is no inbuilt rotation or compression of these log files, and you may want to consider adding one using your tool of choice. Alternatively, there is a Puppet module to manage the log rotate on the Puppet Forge at `https://forge.puppetlabs.com/rodjek/logrotate`.

> If you do relocate the `reports` directory, then ensure that the permissions are set correctly so that the user who runs the Puppet master process has access to both read/write to the reporting directory. If the permissions aren't set correctly, then it can lead to some very weird and wonderful error messages on both the Puppet master and agent.

Now that we understand some of the basics of Puppet reporting, it's time to take a look at the configuration. Let's take another look at the basic configuration that comes out of the box. The configuration file is as follows:

```
[main]
logdir=/var/log/puppet
```

```
vardir=/var/lib/puppet
ssldir=/var/lib/puppet/ssl
rundir=/var/run/puppet
factpath=$vardir/lib/facter
templatedir=$confdir/templates

[master]
# These are needed when the Puppetmaster is run by passenger
# and can safely be removed if webrick is used.
ssl_client_header = SSL_CLIENT_S_DN
ssl_client_verify_header = SSL_CLIENT_VERIFY
```

At this point, no further changes are required on the Puppet master, and it will store client reports by default. However, as mentioned, it will store reports in the `/var/lib/Puppet/reports` directory by default . This isn't ideal in some cases; sometimes, it's impossible to create a `/var` directory that would be big enough (for instance, on hosts that use small primary storage such as SSD drives), or you may wish to place your logs onto a centralized storage space such as an **NFS** share. This is very easy to change, so let's take a look at changing our default configuration to point to a new location. This is described in the following code:

```
[main]
logdir=/var/log/puppet
vardir=/var/lib/puppet
ssldir=/var/lib/puppet/ssl
rundir=/var/run/puppet
factpath=$vardir/lib/facter
templatedir=$confdir/templates

[master]
reportdir = /mnt/puppetreports
# These are needed when the puppetmaster is run by passenger
# and can safely be removed if webrick is used.
ssl_client_header = SSL_CLIENT_S_DN
ssl_client_verify_header = SSL_CLIENT_VERIFY
```

Make sure that once you have created your Puppet's `reports` directory, you change the permissions to match your Puppet user (normally, `puppet:puppet` for Unix and Linux systems) and restart the Puppet master. Go ahead and run the client again, and you should see the report appear in your new reporting directory.

If you're using Puppet Enterprise, then none of this applies; the installer has taken care of this for you. If you take a look at the configuration directory (normally `/etc/Puppetlabs/master`), you can see that the `Puppet.conf` file has the same changes. Puppet Enterprise is configured out of the box to use the HTTP and **PuppetDB** storage method. This is a far more scalable way of doing things than the standard `reportdir` directory and store method, and it is a good example of where Puppet Enterprise is designed with scale in mind. This doesn't mean that you can't do this in the open source version, though; in the following chapters, we will go through setting up Puppet Open Source to use these report processors and more.

Setting up the Puppet agent

Much like the Puppet master, the Puppet agent is configured with sensible default settings out of the box. In fact, in most cases, you will not need to make any changes. The only exception, generally, is if you are using a separate reporting server; in this case, you will need to specify the host that you have assigned this role to.

You can adjust the Puppet agent's reporting behavior using the report setting within the `[agent]` configuration block of the Puppet configuration file. This is a simple Boolean switch that defines the behavior of the Puppet agent during a run, and by default, it is set to `true`. Sometimes, you may find that you wish to explicitly set this to `true` to aid anyone who is less familiar with Puppet. You can safely set this explicitly by making the following code amendment to the `puppet.conf` file:

```
[main]
logdir=/var/log/puppet
vardir=/var/lib/puppet
ssldir=/var/lib/puppet/ssl
rundir=/var/run/puppet
factpath=$vardir/lib/facter
templatedir=$confdir/templates

[master]
# These are needed when the Puppetmaster is run by passenger
# and can safely be removed if webrick is used.
ssl_client_header = SSL_CLIENT_S_DN
ssl_client_verify_header = SSL_CLIENT_VERIFY

And now let's insert the option for the client to report:
[main]
logdir=/var/log/puppet
vardir=/var/lib/puppet
ssldir=/var/lib/puppet/ssl
```

```
rundir=/var/run/puppet
factpath=$vardir/lib/facter
templatedir=$confdir/templates

[agent]
report = true

[master]
# These are needed when the Puppetmaster is run by passenger
# and can safely be removed if webrick is used.
ssl_client_header = SSL_CLIENT_S_DN
ssl_client_verify_header = SSL_CLIENT_VERIFY
```

These are the essentials to configure Puppet in order to report. There are other options available in both the Puppet agent and the Puppet master configuration that are related to reporting, but these are strictly optional; the default settings are generally okay. If you're curious, you can find a complete list of the available options on the Puppet Labs website at `http://docs.puppetlabs.com/references/latest/configuration.html`. Be cautious, though; some of these settings can do some very weird things to your setup and should only be used if you really need them.

Well done; you are now up and running with Puppet reporting, albeit in a very basic form. We could end the book here, but the fun is only just starting. Now that we understand how the Puppet agent interacts with the Puppet master to create reports, we can start to examine some of the other powerful features that Puppet reporting offers us.

Summary

After reading this chapter, you should now appreciate how Puppet goes about its reporting. We explored the Puppet configuration file and observed how both Puppet Enterprise and Puppet Open Source are configured for simple reporting by default. We explored the interaction between the Puppet master and the Puppet agent and looked at how Puppet and Facter work together to create detailed reports of both the activity and state. We also observed that custom facts can be added to any report. We briefly covered scalability by noting that you can use a separate Puppet master to act as a dedicated report server, and we looked at some of the reasons as to why you might want to do this.

In the next chapter, we're going to take a look at some of the dashboards that can be used with Puppet and take a whistle-stop tour of some of the major features that each of them has. You'll see how these dashboards can offer some quick and easy reporting options but also have see of the limitations of using them.

2
Viewing Data in Dashboards

In the previous chapter, we found out how easy it is to make Puppet expose a rich seam of information from the hosts; however, at this point in time, we have no easy way of mining it. In the next few chapters, we are going to look at some of the ways in which we can both extract and interact with the data that Puppet provides, but in the meantime, we will spend a little time going over the tools that are already available. These tools provide a quick and easy out-of-the-box experience, and in the case of Puppet Enterprise and The Foreman, also form a central part of the management tool chain.

In this chapter, we're going to cover the following:

- A brief introduction to dashboards
- A quick tour of Puppet Dashboard and Puppet Enterprise Console
- A brief look at The Foreman
- An introduction to PuppetBoard

Why use a dashboard?

One of the advantages of using Puppet to manage your infrastructure is that it allows you to simplify the management and organization of your nodes and impose order on even the largest pool of resources. This is only one part of the picture, however, and an important element to any kind of system, such as Puppet, is being able to visualize what you manage. A dashboard is shown in the following screenshot:

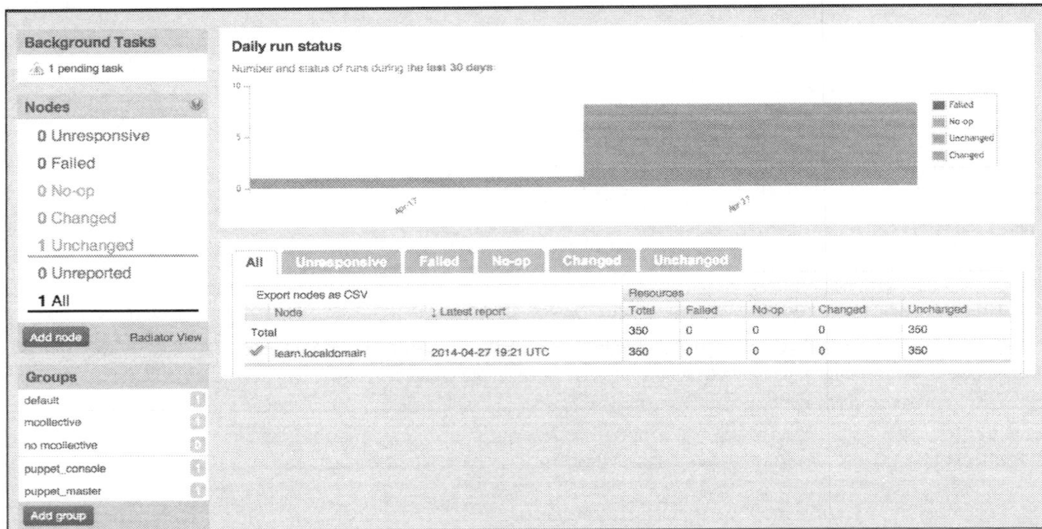

Puppet now has several dashboards available for use, and most of these offer capabilities above and beyond simply reporting data. Most dashboards can also act as **External Node Classifiers (ENCs)**, and in some cases, can drive actions by integrating with MCollective and even form a key part of the server build process if you use The Foreman. Even without utilizing these features, you will find that a dashboard can offer both your users and you a valuable insight into what is happening within your Puppet-managed infrastructure, and will allow you to interrogate the facts and reports returned by the Puppet agents. It's worth noting that in many cases, if you do not use these dashboards as ENCs, you may find that some information will not be accessible. For instance, Puppet Dashboard cannot tell which classes are assigned to a particular node unless it's being used as an ENC.

We are not going to go into a huge amount of detail regarding how to set up each of these products as you can find installation instructions along with the respective projects. If you are a Puppet Enterprise user, then you will find that Puppet Enterprise Console is installed as part of the overall product.

Before going into detail about the dashboards, it's worth looking at the features that each of them can offer. I've summarized this into a table, which is shown as a screenshot in the next section.

The Puppet Dashboard feature list

In the following screenshot, we will identify the feature list available and understand the availability of these features in different dashboards:

	Puppet Dashboard	Puppet Enterprise Console	The Foreman	PuppetBoard
ENC	✔	✔	✔	
Reporting	✔	✔	✔	✔
Class Discovery		✔	✔	
PuppetDB Integration		✔		✔
MCollective Integration		✔		

- **ENC**: This denotes that this dashboard can be utilized as an external node classifier
- **Reporting**: This dashboard can produce reports on a Puppet agent's activity
- **Class Discovery**: This dashboard can examine installed Puppet modules and extract class names for allocation in the ENC
- **PuppetDB Integration**: This dashboard can use PuppetDB as a data source
- **MCollective Integration**: This denotes that this dashboard can use MCollective to orchestrate actions against nodes

Understanding Puppet Dashboard

Puppet Dashboard is the original dashboard that was shipped with Puppet and was designed to provide a graphical ENC and reporting console. Since the advent of Puppet Enterprise, Puppet Labs no longer directly supports the open source version of the dashboard and it is now maintained by the open source community.

Puppet Dashboard fulfills the role of both an ENC and an end point for Puppet reporting. As an ENC, Puppet Dashboard is capable and will allow you to both define classes and assign them to nodes. Note, though, that classes are defined manually, so if you do use Puppet Dashboard as an ENC, you will need to add some new classes to the dashboard if you want to add a new module.

Puppet Dashboard was designed to be simple enough to be read at a glance, and the front page will immediately allow you to see both the number of Puppet agents and which state they reported last in a time series graph along the top of the dashboard. The panel to the left of the graph allows you to see in detail how many nodes have failed to run, are pending changes, have changed, or are unchanged. It also shows you unresponsive and unreported nodes; these are important metrics and well worth keeping an eye on. An unresponsive node is any node that has not reported back in an hour, and it is probably a signifier of issues if you see a large number in this column. You can configure the cutoff period if you tend to run your Puppet agents on a different schedule to the usual 30 minutes. Unreported nodes occur if you commission a node in Puppet Dashboard and it never reports—these are something that should be somewhat of a rarity.

At the bottom of the front page is a table that allows you to see more details of the nodes, with each tab representing a state from the status summary on the left-hand side of the page. In the table, you can see the hostname of the node, the date and time of its last report, and some statistics around how many resources the Puppet agent has either applied, failed to apply, or left unchanged. By clicking on the links in the table, you can explore the report and node further.

The open source Puppet Dashboard is relatively simple to set up and can offer you a reasonable level of reporting. It includes ENC functionality and can be used to categorize and apply classes to your nodes. At the time of writing, however, community participation has been low, and I would not recommend using the open source Puppet Dashboard unless you have a compelling need to. If you do want to install or, better yet, contribute towards Puppet Dashboard, then you can find it at `https://github.com/sodabrew/puppet-dashboard`.

Exploring Puppet Enterprise Console

Puppet Labs have focused their time on improving Puppet Dashboard in the enterprise release of Puppet, and to start to differentiate it from the previous dashboard, they have renamed it Puppet Enterprise Console. Although superficially similar to each other, the two projects have very different offerings. Puppet Enterprise Console offers integration with MCollective, and PuppetDB offers out-of-the-box, enhanced features such as Event Inspector and Live Management. Puppet Enterprise Console forms the core of the enterprise product and offers a central place of management and a solid reporting tool, and increasingly, is the place to orchestrate your infrastructure. This dashboard is shown in the following screenshot:

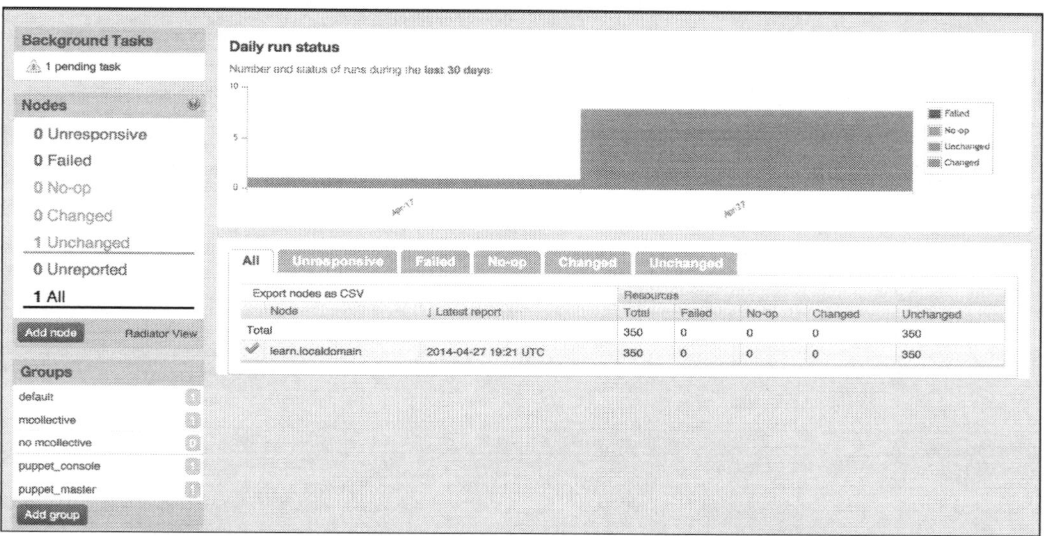

In terms of layout and basic reporting capabilities, Puppet Enterprise Console is very similar to the open source Puppet Dashboard, and if you are migrating from Puppet Dashboard to Puppet Enterprise Console, you should find yourself at home. We're going to take a look at the two major features Puppet Enterprise Console has that sets it apart from its open source progenitor.

Event Inspector

Event Inspector is a relatively new addition to Puppet Enterprise Console, and it gives you a quick and easy way to correlate events between multiple nodes over a certain period of time. This can be seen in the following screenshot:

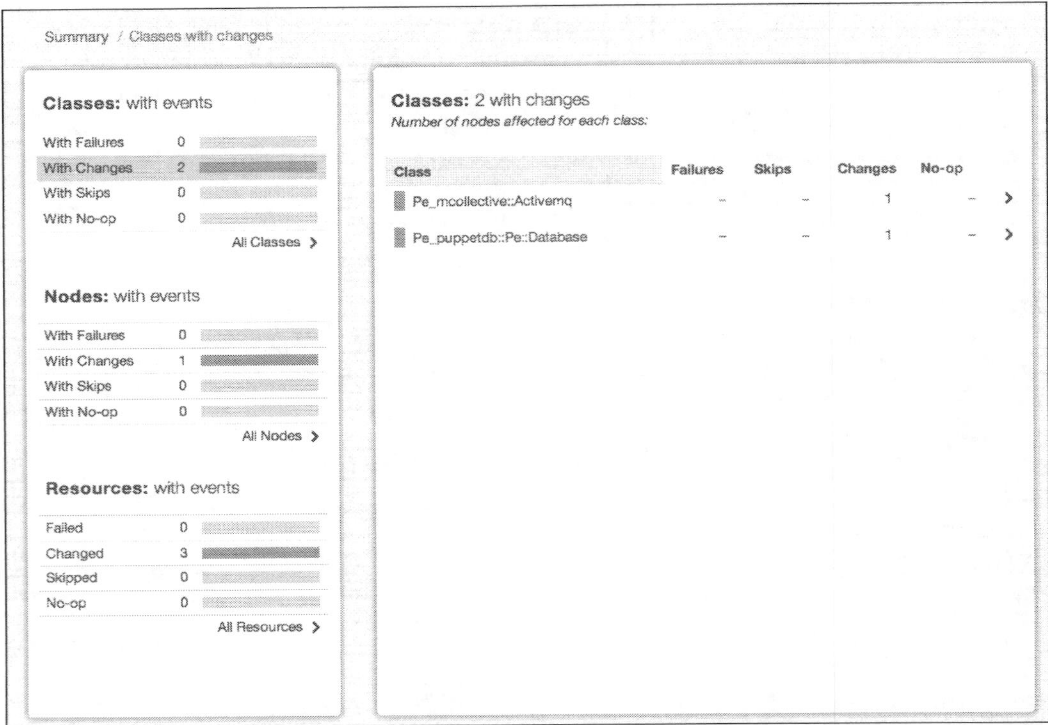

The events console also has a feature called **perspectives**. This allows you to view the data from one of three different ways, from the nodes, classes, or resources perspectives. This ability to flip between views is very useful and quickly allows you to contextualize an event.

For instance, take a failure on a group of nodes. Viewing them from the nodes perspective allows you to see that a group of nodes failed during the previous run. However, flipping over to the classes' perspective shows you that the failure occurred within a particular class; this allows you to quickly zero in on changes that have had an adverse affect on your Puppet-managed infrastructure.

The events console is one of the major differences between the open source and enterprise versions of Puppet, and it gives you an idea of the direction that Puppet Labs is moving in with regards to reporting. You can expect that in future releases of Puppet Enterprise, the reporting gap will only increase.

Puppet Live Management

Puppet Enterprise features integration with another Puppet-Labs-curated product, MCollective (`http://puppetlabs.com/mcollective`). MCollective is an orchestration product that allows you to execute commands in parallel on many nodes, and by integrating MCollective into Puppet Enterprise Console, Puppet Labs has created a new feature called Puppet Live Management. This can be seen in the following screenshot:

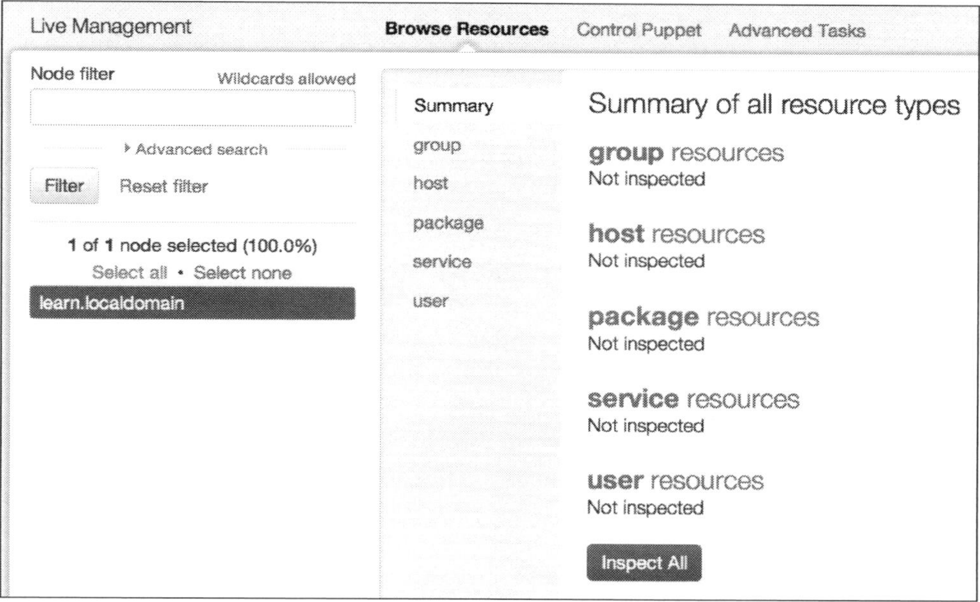

Puppet Live Management allows you to control Puppet on your nodes from the comfort of your Puppet Enterprise Console application. For instance, if you've pushed a change on a Puppet module and can't wait for the usual 30 minutes for it to take effect, you can use Puppet Enterprise Console to do a one-off Puppet run on a node or even a group of nodes. Likewise, you can enable and disable the Puppet agent, plus find its status on all the managed nodes.

Puppet Live Management is not just limited to managing Puppet agents, though; it can leverage MCollective plugins to further enhance its capabilities. A fresh installation of Puppet Enterprise Console has preinstalled plugins that allow you to carry out tasks such as package installation and restarting services, and these can be further supplemented with any available MCollective plugin.

Puppet Enterprise Console is the evolution of the open source Puppet Dashboard and is increasingly differentiating itself with new and exciting features. It is, however, only available if you use Puppet Enterprise and cannot be split off as a separate product. You can download Puppet Enterprise Console along with Puppet Enterprise from `http://puppetlabs.com/puppet/puppet-enterprise`.

Using The Foreman

The Foreman is an open source project that is, in its own words, a life cycle management tool. Rather than being limited to acting as an ENC for Puppet, The Foreman can also provide unattended installation facilities for kickstart, jumpstart, and preseed-based systems. This essentially means that The Foreman is able to create our system from its initial boot, through first configuration, and then manage its state for the rest of its life cycle. This dashboard is shown in the following screenshot:

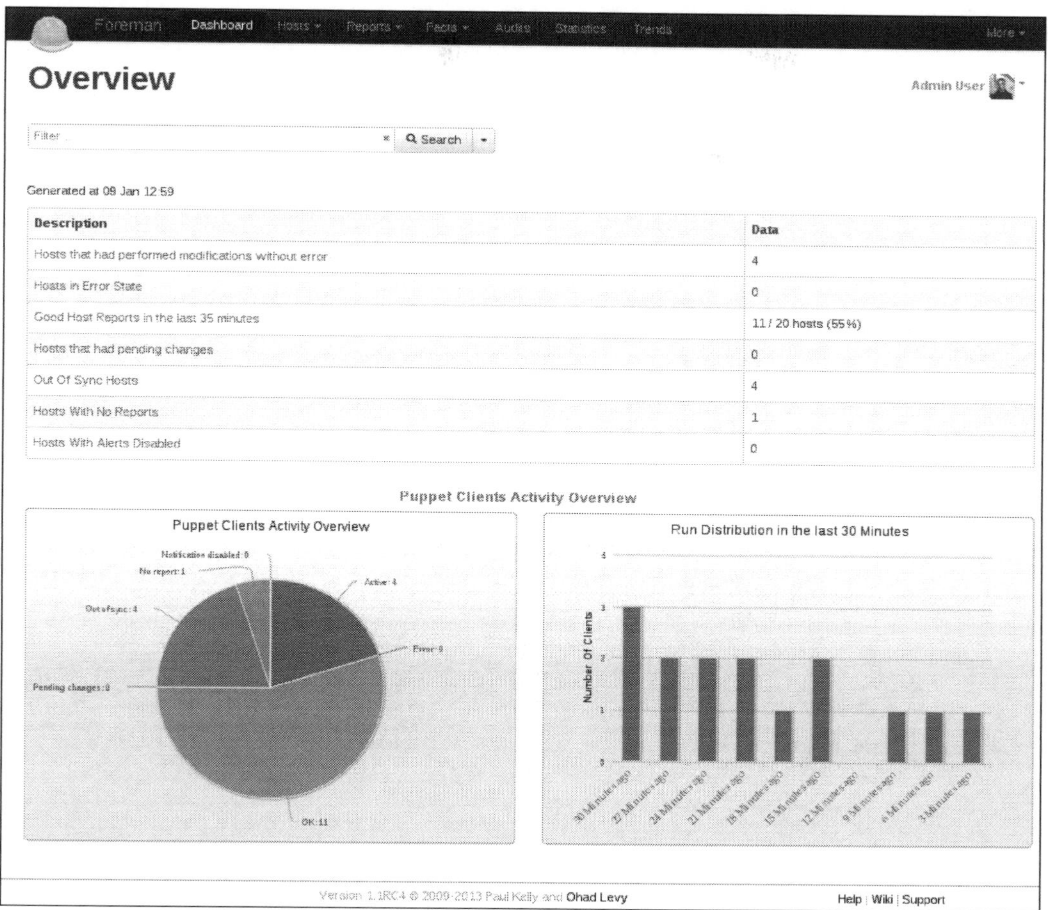

From the point of view of reporting, The Foreman offers much the same as Puppet Dashboard, including the ability to view individual host details and reports. However, it also has some of its own interesting tricks. The Foreman has put an awful lot of thought behind reporting and has two standout features: trends and audits. These offer a unique view of our Puppet-managed infrastructure and are exceptionally powerful reporting tools.

Reporting with The Foreman

Reporting forms a very large part of The Foreman feature set, and The Foreman is possibly the most capable out of each of the dashboards in this regard. Not only is The Foreman able to report the usual details, such as facts and reports from nodes, but it is also able to create full audit reports for them (who made what change to which servers) that are well presented and make heavy use of charts to ensure that the data is clear and easy to read. The Foreman also has an interesting feature to look at historical data called trends.

Looking at trends in The Foreman

The Foreman is able to report on facts, much like other dashboards; however, it also records changes in state into its own data store. This allows it to build up a view of how facts are trending over time. A good example is to look at the RAM allocated to a certain group of nodes. Using The Foreman trends feature, it is possible to look at how this has grown over time and can be a fantastic aid when trying to work out capacity management problems. Alternatively, any fact that is reported to The Foreman can be viewed as a trend, and this is a fantastic feature that other dashboards currently lack.

The Foreman is a very impressive dashboard for Puppet and well worth considering, especially if you need a quick and powerful reporting solution. It works best when it is acting as the Puppet ENC, however, so if you install and use it simply as a reporting tool, you may find that some features do not work as expected.

Discovering PuppetBoard

PuppetBoard is a relatively young product, and as such, may have a few rough edges; however, despite its youth, it already offers an excellent interface for reporting. PuppetBoard uses PuppetDB as its data source, and aside from Puppet Enterprise Console, it is the only product to do so. PuppetBoard eschews any ambition of forming part of the management layer, and instead, it focuses on providing a clear and easy-to-use reporting feature. This dashboard is shown in the following screenshot:

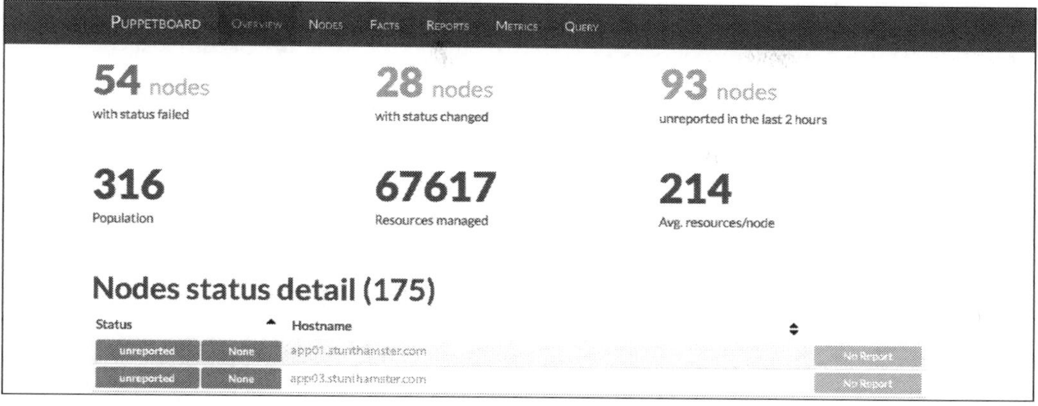

Since PuppetBoard is based around PuppetDB, it allows access to all data within it, such as facts and Puppet agent reports and metrics. It allows you to explore this data intuitively using an easy-to-use interface. PuppetBoard allows you to explore the data held in PuppetDB from the point of view of nodes, facts, and reports, and it also allows you to drill through each element to explore further details. For instance, by drilling into a node, you are able to see its connected facts and reports, and by drilling into facts, you are able to see the nodes connected to that particular fact along with an appropriate graph. The **FACTS** view is particularly useful as it not only lists each node with the associated fact value, but also presents it neatly in the form of a graph. This can be invaluable for quickly gauging the rollout of operating systems, for instance. This is described in the following screenshot:

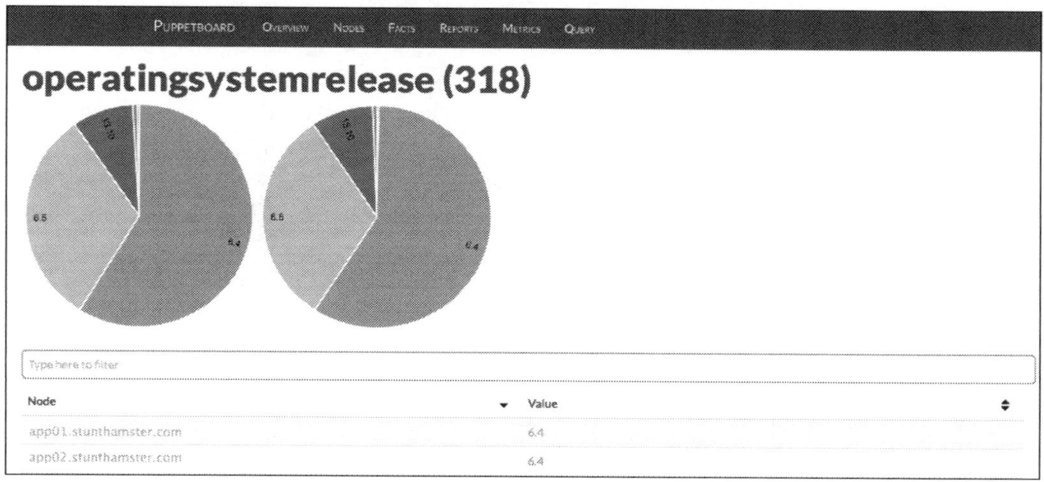

The other useful feature is the query panel. This allows you to run freeform PuppetDB queries utilizing the PuppetDB query API. So, if a particular view of data is not present in the predefined PuppetBoard reports, you can quickly make up ad hoc ones. We will explore PuppetDB and its query API in *Chapter 6, Retrieving Data with the PuppetDB API*.

PuppetBoard is a young project, but it is extremely promising even at this early stage. If you use Hiera or some other way to classify nodes, then PuppetBoard is an excellent addition to your Puppet infrastructure as it does not require that Puppet agents use it as an ENC for any of its features. Combine this with easy-to-use reporting and a relatively lightweight installation and you have the makings of an excellent dashboard. You can find the code and installation instructions for PuppetBoard at `https://github.com/nedap/puppetboard`.

Summary

You should now be aware of which dashboards are available for Puppet and what features they can offer you. As you can see, they can add a fantastic insight into the running of your Puppet infrastructure without needing to expend much effort. Using these dashboards gives you quick and easy access to both your Puppet reports and gathered data from your hosts via Facter, and they can be used to easily track changes over time. There are problems, though. First of all, you need to use these panels as an ENC to leverage their full power. Without this, you can use the majority of the reporting features, but they will still be missing certain elements. They are also inflexible, with almost no opportunity to customize the reports to suit your purposes, and in some cases, their development is lagging.

In the next chapter, you will learn how to create your own report processors. Report processors form a key part of Puppet reporting and will start you on the way to producing your own reports and alerts.

3

Introducing Report Processors

In the previous chapters, we looked at some of the basic steps needed to enable Puppet reporting and learned how to view some of the data that the Puppet agents produce. In this chapter, we will learn how to enable the Puppet master to process these reports and metrics using report processors. We will cover the following topics:

- Basics of report processors
- Default report processors that ship with Puppet
- How to send Puppet alerts with Twitter
- Using **PagerDuty** to log and escalate issues

Report processors form the heart of Puppet reporting; so, it's important that you get a good grounding in what they are, what they can do, and how you can go about adding new ones. Once you've got a good grasp of how they are installed and confi,gured, you will be amazed at some of the additional functionality that a good report processor can add to Puppet, not just for producing reports, but also for raising alerts and more.

Understanding a report processor

It's one thing to be able to gather data, but it's quite another thing to then be able to do anything interesting with it. Having data without any means of access is simply wasting disk space and bandwidth. It's been the bane of many systems that they seem to gather lots of data and then make it tooth-grindingly frustrating to get any kind of sensible access to it. Puppet has been designed from the outset to make it easy for you to gather and access any data that it collects, both by using open source data formats and by providing a plugin system in the form of report processors that allow you to process that data.

Report processors are pieces of Ruby code that are placed within Puppet's `lib` directory and are treated as plugins. When a report processor is enabled, the Puppet master will pass the YAML data it receives from the Puppet agents into the report processor every time a Puppet agent completes a transaction. It is then up to that particular plugin to do something interesting with the data, and as it's a straightforward piece of Ruby code, you can let your imagination run riot! If you can do it in Ruby, you can do it with a report processor; and if you can't do it in Ruby, you can easily write a report processor to forward the data to a data processing weapon of your choice.

Puppet does not limit you to one report plugin; you can have as many as you like installed at any given time. You need to keep in mind that these plugins are being executed on your Puppet master, and you need to ensure that the report processor(s) does not leave the Puppet master process starved of resources. There are various techniques that can be used to move data into other systems, and in this chapter and others, we will explore some of the ways of doing that. One of the simplest ways to scale Puppet reporting is to add another Puppet master for reporting. As we explored in *Chapter 1, Setting Up Puppet for Reporting*, it's easy to add a Puppet master dedicated to reporting, and this is highly recommended as a scaling technique. There is no reason that this server needs to be the actual reporting Puppet master either; you could potentially use a **load balancer** to enable several reporting Puppet master servers in the frontend.

It is exceptionally useful to have the ability to install multiple report processors. You could potentially have one script that deals with errors and sends alerts to the correct person, another plugin that creates some lovely graphs of your Puppet activity, and finally (and I have seen this), a report processor that alerts an Arduino board to play the James Bond theme if certain terms are seen. It can't be overstated how powerful the reporting subsystem can potentially be; Puppet is probably one of the few systems that has almost complete knowledge of your infrastructure, from how many CPU cores a node has to how a piece of software is configured. Add in some suitable custom facts and there's almost nothing you cannot find out with Puppet, and once Puppet knows about it, a report processor can act on it.

Report processors are installed in the `$vardir/Puppet/reports` directory within Puppet's `install` directory and only need to be present on the Puppet master. The Puppet agent neither knows nor cares what happens to the data; it simply sends it to the Puppet master for processing. That being said, it doesn't matter if the report processors are present on the Puppet agents as they will never be called on the agent side.

It's worth noting that prior to Puppet Version 3.3.0, the report format was a YAML document. From Version 3.3.0 onwards, it now uses a PSON-formatted document (a variant of JSON). Generally speaking, this shouldn't matter too much for our purposes, but it is worth knowing in case you use firewalls that have blocks based on the content type. You can use the `report_serialization_format` option within the `puppet.conf` configuration if you need to set it back to the legacy YAML format.

There are two ways in which you can install a report processor. The most traditional and, in some ways, straightforward method is to copy the code and place it on your Puppet master. This is completely supported by Puppet, simple to carry out, and has the advantage of being quick; however, it lacks a certain elegance and is not really in keeping with the Puppet spirit of automation.

A more refined way to install report processors is to package them inside a Puppet module. The module itself simply needs a `/lib/puppet/reports` directory for your shiny new plugin code to be placed. You'll also need a blank `init.pp` file in the `manifests` directory to ensure that Puppet has something to run. Once the module is installed on the Puppet master, you just need to perform a Puppet client run. Thanks to the magic of Puppet's plugin sync mechanism (which is enabled by default since Puppet Version 3), you will find that the new report processor is installed in the correct location with the correct ownership and permissions.

This installation method may seem counterintuitive at first, but it makes complete sense to do it this way. By following this convention, it becomes much easier to distribute your code. It simplifies building new Puppet masters with Puppet and ensures that if you release a new version, it will be automatically propagated and updated. Another major benefit is that by producing a report processor as a module, it makes it easier for you to submit it to Puppet Forge for other people to make use of your work.

Puppet Forge is a fantastic repository of Puppet modules written by both Puppet Labs themselves and the community at large. As long as you follow the pattern of using a module to distribute your code, you can add it to Puppet Forge. By adding your code to Puppet Forge, you are not only sharing your expertise and code with other Puppet users, but you are also allowing them to improve upon these codes. After reading this book, you may have some fantastic ideas for a report processor, and it would be fantastic for you to share it on Puppet Forge. You can view the existing modules as well as sign up to publish your own at `https://forge.puppetlabs.com`.

We'll come back to the organizational and developmental aspects of report processors in *Chapter 4, Creating Your Own Report Processor*. For now, let's take a look at some of the existing report processors available in Puppet.

Utilizing the built-in report processors

Puppet ships with several report processors that have already been included, and they offer some fairly fantastic capabilities right away without needing to write a single line of code. The included plugins cover a fairly wide spectrum of requirements, from storing the raw reports to sending alerts via e-mail based on certain criteria. The included report processors are the following:

- store
- report
- rrdgraph
- tagmail
- HTTP
- PuppetDB

Over the next few pages, we're going to take a look at these built-in report processors and what they are capable of. You are going to find that the included report processors offer a rather impressive range of abilities and can immediately offer you not only better insight into your infrastructure, but also some new and interesting alerting abilities.

Storing reports with the store report processor

The store report processor is the simplest report processor packaged with Puppet, and it does exactly what it says on the tin; it takes incoming reports and stores them to a location on a disk. It is also the default report processor to be used if you enable reporting on the Puppet master.

Although it sounds simple, this processor is incredibly versatile, as the file it creates is a complete dump of the report data from the Puppet agent. This ensures that every part of the `puppet::transaction::report` object is stored, including the log, metrics, and resources. This is something that other report processors may not necessarily do as there is a very large difference between processing log data and processing metrics. Possibly the biggest asset of the store report processor is that it allows for the option of ingesting the files into a separate analytical tool such as Crystal Reports or any other data analysis tool. The store report processor lends itself nicely to producing data for batch processing, and it should be the first place to look if you are dealing with the batch capture and transform tools for analysis.

Configuring the store report processor is straightforward. To enable it, you simply need to edit the `puppet.conf` file and add the following lines of code:

```
[master]
reports = store
reportstore = /var/log/Puppet
```

Once you've added these lines of code, you'll need to restart the Puppet master process. Although Puppet will automatically reload its configuration when a change is made, the report processor is not automatically started; so, to ensure that any new reporting configuration changes are picked up, it's best to remain in the habit of restarting the Puppet master when you make any changes.

The first line of the preceding code snippet tells the Puppet master to load the store report processor, and the second line then tells the processor where to store the processed files. As long as you've left the clients for reporting in their default setting, you should find that your `reports` directory starts to fill up with reports.

Remember to keep an eye on your disk space usage on the partition the reports are being stored on; although each report is quite small on its own, the reports soon start adding up. If you're using an application of your own devise to crunch the data, you may want to consider either removing the data post processing or, at the very least, archiving it into some form of compressed file. The Puppet master has no further interaction with the data, so either removing the stored reports or compressing them will have no effect on the running of your Puppet master.

Adding to logfiles with the log report processor

The log report processor is, in some ways, similar to the store report processor. Rather than storing the report on a disk with the Puppet master, the log report processor sends it to the local syslog server for logging. This can be enormous fun when coupled with a remote syslog server and can make collecting reports from multiple Puppet masters a complete breeze. This is especially useful if you are running a large or complex Puppet installation as it allows you to have a single place to look for issues rather than having to look at individual servers.

To enable the log report processor, you can add the following code snippet to the `puppet.conf` file:

```
[master]
reports = log
```

That's it; no configuration is required as all this processor does is hand the data to the underlying syslog system; it's up to you to configure your syslog to deal with the data in an appropriate manner by adding syslog filters and log rotation rules. This is out of the scope of this book, but it should be covered by your syslog tools' documentation. At the least, you will probably want some kind of rule in place to split the Puppet master data into a separate log file, as a busy infrastructure will easily drown out any other messages that go to the default syslog; such a rule will also make it easier to manage the data from a housekeeping point of view. Much like the store report processor, the log report processor can log a surprisingly large amount of data in a short time, so you'll almost certainly want a daily rotation and compression housekeeping task.

Graphing with the rrdgraph processor

RRD stands for **Round Robin Database**, and it is an industry standard graphing format used by everything from routers to monitoring services and everything in between. The RRD format is widely used and recognized by many different applications that will allow you to present the data in interesting and attractive ways. An example graph is shown in the following screenshot:

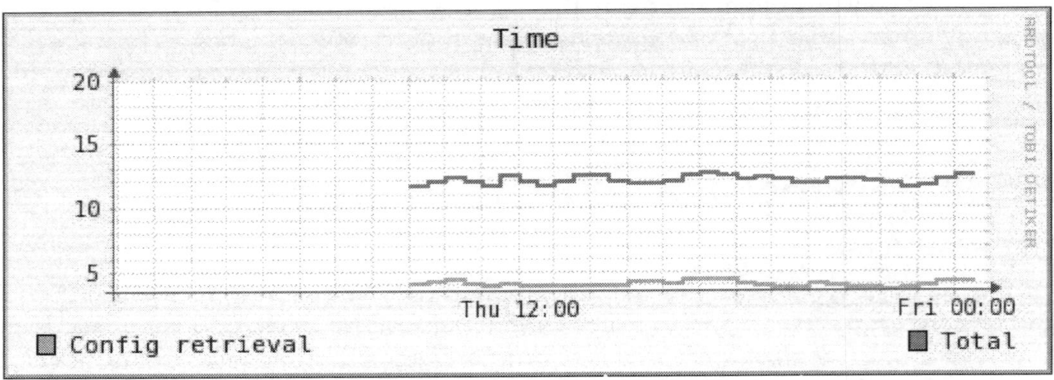

The rrdgraph plugin is arguably one of the most useful report processors that ships with Puppet, and even without additional components, it will allow you to produce some wonderful graphs of the Puppet activity with minimal effort. This can be especially useful if you are either unable or unwilling to run one of the Puppet dashboards. Many of the graphs produced by the dashboards can be replicated using the rrdgraph report processor, and although the output is not as attractive or easy to use, it's still very usable and informative.

Once installed, the rrdgraph report processor will produce a set of graphs that outline the important metrics from the data passed to it by the Puppet agents. The way it produces and stores the graphs is fantastically useful and very easy to work with. Every time the rrdgraph report processor is run, it will produce a directory for each host that reports to the Puppet master. Inside the directory, you will find an `.html` file that, when opened, will present the graphs. Voila! A kind of instant dashboard is created.

Along with producing graphs, the rrdgraph report processor will also give you the raw RRD data used to create the graphs. This is great, as it means that you can plug it into any other application that understands RRD data, and that's a lot of applications! By using a networked filesystem or some other method of syncing the data, you can make the RRD data available to these applications pretty much in real time. This can be incredibly useful if you already have an application that makes use of the RRD data to build up a business or infrastructure dashboard as it means that Puppet can be plugged straight into it.

Although the rrdgraph plugin is distributed with Puppet, it relies on other software and libraries that may not necessarily be preinstalled on your system. This is common with more complex report processors, as they tend to rely on other components to do some of the heavy lifting or communicate with other systems, either in the form of additional packages offered by the OS, or more commonly, via the RubyGems packaging system.

In the case of the rrdgraph report processor, the first additional package you'll want to install are the RRD tools themselves; the exact installation method will vary from distro to distro. To install it on Debian-based distributions, you can use the following command at the command prompt:

```
apt-get install rrdtool
```

For RedHat-based distributions, you can use the following command:

```
yum install rrdtool
```

You will also need the Ruby RRD libraries. These should ship with your distribution and can be installed in the usual manner. If you are using a Debian-based distribution, you can install it using the following command:

```
$ apt-get install librrd-ruby
```

If you are using a RedHat-based distribution, you can install it using the following command:

```
$ yum install rrdtool-ruby
```

Once the prerequisite components are installed, make the following addition to the `puppet.conf` file:

```
[master]
reports = rrdgraph
rrddir = $vardir/rrd
rrdgraph = true
```

The extra configuration items are important. The `rrddir` object tells Puppet which directory it should output the graphs to. If you want to quickly and easily see the data, then make sure that this is a directory that a web server is able to read, and this way, you can access it straightaway in your browser and admire the pretty graphs.

The other object in the preceding code is `rrdgraph`. This is a simple Boolean setting that controls the production of the actual graphs. If you're going to feed the data into another system, you may just want Puppet to produce the RRD data without requiring the graphs, and this setting will allow you to turn this behavior on or off. By default, this is set to `true`.

The tagmail report processor

The tagmail report processor is a quick and easy way to get Puppet to send e-mails, and it is clever enough to do this based on certain criteria you give it. The tagmail report processor works via the magic of Puppet tags, a particularly underappreciated Puppet feature.

Puppet tagging is a way to mark out elements within Puppet, allowing you to identify individual resources or classes. What's nice is that Puppet will automatically do this for you to some extent. By default, Puppet will automatically tag every resource that it successfully parses and will make available the following tags:

- The resource type
- The full name of the class in which the resource is declared
- Every segment of the namespace of the resource class

This is brilliant as it gives you a very rich set of tags to work with without lifting a finger. You can also manually tag resources within your Puppet code if you wish to add clarity or order, and this is something that I would encourage. So how does this fit into the tagmail report processor?

Let's say you have a very important set of nodes that utilize a certain class, and you want to be informed every time that the Puppet agent applies or interacts with resources in that class. Using the tagmail report processor, this becomes very easy; simply identify the resources that you're interested in and the tagmail report processor will inform you via an e-mail when something has happened to them.

To tell the report processor what tags you are interested in, you need to build a tag map. A tag map is a very simple configuration file that contains all of the Puppet tags that you want to match and the e-mail address that should receive the notification. You can also use exclusionary rules to start building up some simple logic around your Puppet tags. Take a look at the following code example:

```
all: ops@fictionalco.com
web,webops@fictionalco.com, ops@fictionalco.com
tomcat, !jboss: javadevs@fictionalco.com
```

It's as simple as that. The preceding example will do the following things:

- Send an e-mail every time the processors see any tag. This will send you an e-mail every time a Puppet agent runs and is generally a bit verbose for everyday use.
- Send the WebOps and Ops teams an e-mail when a Puppet agent applies a resource that uses the `web` Puppet tag.
- Send the Javadevs team an e-mail if the Puppet agent applies a resource that contains a `tomcat` tag but not if it also contains a `jboss` tag.

The following Puppet code snippet can demonstrate how these tags are set:

```
class role::public_web {
   nginx::vhost{'blog':
      hostname => 'myblog.com',
      tag      => 'web',
}

   tomcat::connector {'appa':
      port => 8080,
      tag  => 'tomcat',
   }

   jboss::connector {'appb':
      port => 8081,
```

```
        tag  => 'jboss',
    }

    user: {'appserver':
        username =>'appserver',
        tag      =>['jboss', 'tomcat'],
    }
```

In this case, the `ops@fictionalco.com` address would have received an e-mail simply because any resource has been applied. The `webops@fictionalco.com` address would have received an e-mail about the `nginx` vhost being applied as it is tagged as a `web` item. Finally, the `javadevs@fictionalco.com` address would have received an e-mail regarding the `jboss` connector resource. Note our user would not have received any e-mail about the `user` resource as it contains the `tomcat` tag.

Using resource tags is useful and will allow you to quickly and easily put together some basic e-mail alerts for the resources that you are interested in. However, one of the quickest and easiest things you can do with the tagmail report processor is configure it to warn you of the potential problems with Puppet. The tagmail report processor parses log-level data within the Puppet report as additional tags. This enables it to react to events that are warnings, errors, or indeed any other log levels available. Take a look at the following tag map code:

```
err: ops@fictonalco.com
```

Once this line is added, every time the processor encounters a tag of `err`, it will send you an e-mail; or, to put it another way, every time one of your nodes has problems applying a Puppet manifest, you will receive an e-mail that will warn you about the issue.

It is a straightforward task to configure the tagmail plugin, and aside from the `tagmap` file, it has no other external dependencies. To enable it, simply add the following code to your `puppet.conf` file:

```
[master]
reports = tagmail
tagmap = $confdir/tagmap.conf
```

The preceding code is fairly self explanatory; the first line enables the tagmail report processor and the second line tells it where it can find its tag map. Note the use of the `$conf` variable in front of the `tagmap.conf` file; this will point Puppet to its own `config` directory to find the `tagmap` file. It's generally sensible to keep the report processor configuration alongside your main line Puppet configuration, but if you want to put it elsewhere, you can. As with the other plugins, you'll need to restart the Puppet master process for the plugin to take effect.

You can find the documentation for tags at `http://docs.puppetlabs.com/puppet/latest/reference/lang_tags.html` and the documentation for tagmail report processor configuration at `http://docs.puppetlabs.com/puppet/latest/reference/config_file_tagmail.html`. It's worth reading through both, and they should give you some ideas on how you can add Puppet tags to best utilize this feature.

Sending reports with the HTTP report processor

The HTTP report processor is very much an enabler of other tools. It takes the output of a Puppet transaction report and sends it via HTTP or HTTPS to a URL as a raw YAML file. The application that receives this data is then free to process it in a manner it chooses. This is astoundingly useful as it gives you a quick and easy way to make Puppet communicate with other systems.

Puppet Dashboard, Puppet Enterprise Console, and The Foreman already rely on the HTTP report processor to allow Puppet agents to communicate new data. The HTTP report processor is generally the first place you should look if you need to integrate Puppet with another system. Whatever system you use must be able to process the data that the Puppet agent will pass to it. This data is a YAML file dump of the `puppet::transaction::report` object, so it contains all the data generated by the Puppet agent during a transaction, from reports to metrics.

A good example where you may want to export the data could be change management. Using the HTTP report processor and a tailored application, it would be possible to give the change managers a real-time view of what has changed, when it changed, and where it changed. If they already have such a system, it may be possible to use the HTTP report processor to interact with it.

It is a straightforward task to configure the HTTP report processor. Again, you simply edit your `puppet.conf` file and add the following lines of code:

```
report = http
reporturl = http://Puppetendpoint.fictionalco.com
```

That's it. Now, every time a Puppet agent performs any transaction, the HTTP report processor will forward a YAML document that contains the report to the end point you've configured in the `reporturl` configuration item.

Generally, one of the quickest and easiest ways to integrate Puppet with other systems is to use the HTTP report processor, and as mentioned, it is already in use by Puppet Dashboard, Puppet Enterprise Console, and The Foreman. Any systems that boast of Puppet integration will almost certainly make use of this either in part or as a whole to deliver the integration.

The PuppetDB report processor

We're not going to spend too much time on the PuppetDB report processor as we'll be covering this in much more detail in *Chapter 5, Exploring PuppetDB*. Suffice to say, this report processor forwards the reporting information to PuppetDB for storage. Like the other report processors, all it requires is the following simple addition to the `puppet.conf` file to activate it:

```
[master]
report = puppetdb
```

Without a working PuppetDB installation, this won't be of much use, however. Don't worry though; we'll cover how to set up and use PuppetDB in subsequent chapters.

Exploring the power of third-party plugins

As you can see, the built-in report processors are fantastically useful, but they can only do so much; the tagmail report processor might not format the data in the way you like, or you might have a cool idea for your data but don't want to have to create a web service for the HTTP report processor to push it to. Fortunately, it is very easy indeed to add additional report processors to Puppet. The Puppet reporting system has been designed so that you can plug any number of report processors into it simply and easily, and there are already a small number of additional report processors available that you can install and utilize. A good place to find additional report processors is Puppet Forge; you should find quite a few if you simply search for *report*.

We're going to take a look at some examples of third-party report processors and show you how easy it is to install them.

Getting social with Twitter

Twitter has, for some considerable time, been the destination of choice for any up and coming writer who enjoys the challenge of a word count; a really tiny word count. At 140 characters, it's unlikely that the next great novel will be written using Twitter, but it has blossomed to be one of the number one sites for people to quickly update their followers of their comings and goings. It has turned out to be a wonderfully easy way to stay in touch with friends, family, and casual acquaintances in a way that the more verbose Google+ or Facebook haven't quite managed.

Twitter is also a fantastic way to alert you of issues. It's small, terse, and these days, clients are available for pretty much any device you care to mention. In many ways, Twitter is an excellent replacement for the old-fashioned pager system and has the advantage over SMSes of not needing a cellular connection to receive alerts. Many times, I've been stuck in buildings with no mobile phone signal but an excellent wireless connection to the Internet. The SMSes stopped, but the tweets kept on coming, and there have been occasions where I would have been blissfully unaware of alerts without this additional means of notification.

Because of the public nature of Twitter, there can be some concern that you may be leaking potentially sensitive data. However, as long as you take the precaution of making your Puppet Twitter account private, you can be fairly sure that only people you have allowed to follow will see it. I'm going to go ahead and assume that you have set up a Twitter account for Puppet; however, if you haven't, you can go ahead and create an account at `http://www.twitter.com`.

Installing the Twitter plugin is simple as it has been made available on the Puppet Forge site as a Puppet module, which means that the plugin sync mechanism will take care of the tedious work of installing the report processor plugin for us. Because it's published on Puppet Forge, it means we can also use the built-in Puppet module tool to install the module itself. Simply use the following command on your Puppet master:

```
$ puppetmodule install jamtur01/twitter
```

Once the module is installed, you'll need to go ahead and run the Puppet agent on the Puppet master; this will trigger the plugin sync to install the new plugin in the correct location.

This is not all we need to do, though. Much like the rrdgraph plugin, the Twitter report processor has some additional dependencies and setup that are required for it to work. These are the OAuth and Twitter RubyGems dependencies, and they are required for authentication and communication with the Twitter API. You can install these via RubyGems using the following command:

```
$ sudo gem install oauth twitter
```

Once the dependencies are installed, you will then need to allow the API access from your report processor to your Twitter user. This is relatively straightforward; go to `http://dev.twitter.com/apps/new` and sign in with the user created for your Puppet Twitter account. Once signed in, you'll be asked to fill in a small form that will ask for some details about your application; these should be fairly self-explanatory, but make sure that the access rights are set to read/write or the report processor will be unable to tweet. Once you've completed the questions, you'll be taken to the page for your new application and you'll be given your consumer key and secret. Make note of these; you'll need them in the next step.

The author of the Twitter report processor has provided a small script to generate the settings file. Navigate to the installed Twitter module and you will find a Ruby file called `poauth.rb`. This is shown in the following screenshot:

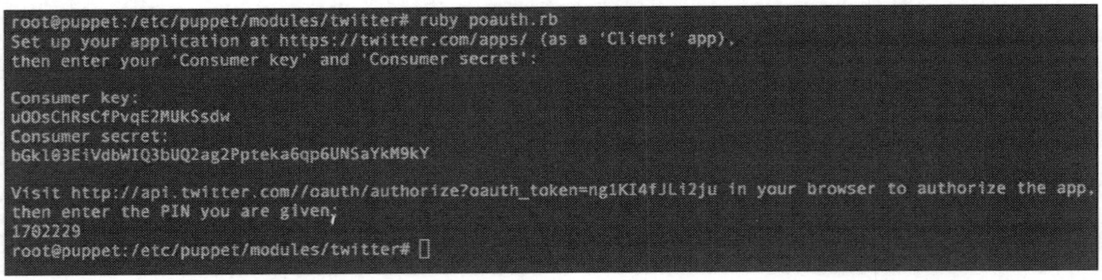

```
root@puppet:/etc/puppet/modules/twitter# ruby poauth.rb
Set up your application at https://twitter.com/apps/ (as a 'Client' app),
then enter your 'Consumer key' and 'Consumer secret':

Consumer key:
uOOsChRsCfPvqE2MUkSsdw
Consumer secret:
bGkl03EiVdbWIQ3bUQ2ag2Ppteka6qp6UNSaYkM9kY

Visit http://api.twitter.com//oauth/authorize?oauth_token=ng1KI4fJLi2ju in your browser to authorize the app,
then enter the PIN you are given:
1702229
root@puppet:/etc/puppet/modules/twitter# 
```

You'll be prompted to enter the consumer key and the secret that you made note of earlier. If you need to remind yourself, you can log in to your Twitter developer account and retrieve it from there. Once you've entered your consumer key and secret, you will be given a unique URL to visit, and the script will wait for you to enter a pin number. Visit the provided URL to receive the pin, and once you've entered it, the script will exit and write out a `twitter.yaml` config file. The Twitter plugin follows convention and expects the configuration file in the Puppet `config` directory, so make sure that you copy the `twitter.yaml` file there once you're finished with the `poauth.rb` script.

You should now have a shiny new API-enabled Twitter user, so the next step is to configure Puppet to use the Twitter plugin. This is a simple configuration change in the `puppet.conf` file to enable reporting in the usual manner, as shown in the following code snippet:

```
[master]
reports = twitter
```

Once you've amended the configuration file and restarted the Puppet master, any failed Puppet client will trigger an alert to Twitter. Now there's no escaping the alerts!

Staying on top of alerts with PagerDuty

PagerDuty is a fantastic tool to record, alert, and escalate issues, and is insanely popular with DevOps folks due to its ease of use and surprising amount of power. Like most modern software, as a service, it's clean and simple to use and has an extremely approachable and powerful API.

PagerDuty is a great place to flag Puppet errors as it gives you the ability to track how often you are having Puppet-related issues. More importantly, it ensures that an alert is created when issues are found. These issues can automatically be escalated to the appropriate person, and if they're out of hours, they can be routed to whoever is on call. PagerDuty supports alerts via phone, SMS, e-mail, and push alerts, so it's unlikely that they'll be able to sleep through a problem. If they do manage to sleep through the sound of every communication device they own going nuts, then PagerDuty is able to alert the issue to the next person on rotation, and it will continue to escalate the issue until someone acknowledges it.

I'm going to assume that you already have a PagerDuty account; if you haven't got one, you can sign up for a free trial at `http://www.pagerduty.com`.

As with the Twitter report processor, the PagerDuty report processor has been published on the Puppet Forge as a module, so we're going to go ahead and use the Puppet module tool to install it. This can be done using the following command:

```
$ puppetmodule install jamtur01/pagerduty
```

Once the module is installed, run the Puppet agent to move the plugin into place. You'll also need to install the rest-client, JSON, and redphone RubyGems dependencies for the processor to be able to communicate with PagerDuty. This can be done using the following command:

```
$sudo gem install rest-client json redphone
```

Once the plugin is installed, we need to let it know what your PagerDuty API key is. You set this by editing the `pagerduty.yaml` file within the PagerDuty module. Open it up using your editor of choice, find the line that starts with `pagerduty_api`, and add your API key to it (you can find this within your PagerDuty account details). You will also need to create a generic service within PagerDuty to receive any alerts.

The final step is to enable the PagerDuty report processor on your Puppet master. As usual, this is a simple change to the `puppet.conf` file on the Puppet master. This is shown in the following code snippet:

```
[master]
reports = pagerduty
```

Restart the Puppet master and you will find that every time Puppet reports an error, an issue will be raised within PagerDuty. This will now e-mail, SMS, and generally bug the person who is responsible for resolving the error. I've found that nothing makes someone fix a bug quicker than having a robot harass them constantly on the phone at unwelcome hours in the morning.

Adding additional report processors to Puppet can make a huge difference to its capabilities. You can find additional report processors listed at Puppet Forge; simply search for the report processors and you should find some. At the time of writing this, there aren't many, but the ones that are available can add some seriously interesting abilities to your Puppet infrastructure. With the available third-party report processors, it becomes relatively simple to make Puppet talk to products such as New Relic, Cube, OpsGenie, and even MCollective, cover capabilities from straightforward reporting to alerting, and even include remedial actions.

Summary

You should now have a good idea of what a report processor is, what it can be used for, and how to install new ones from Puppet Forge. In this chapter, we have examined some of the basic elements of a report processor and discovered that a report processor is a piece of Ruby code that is called every time a Puppet agent reports a transaction. We have found that report processors are easy to install, especially if they are distributed as a Puppet module, but some of the more complex report processors may need to have additional components installed to support them. We also found that you can have multiple report processors configured at once to allow you greater flexibility when processing your data. Finally, we looked at some interesting third-party report processors and used them to interact with products such as PagerDuty and Twitter.

In the next chapter, we are going to look at how to create our own report processors and how we can use our own code to create custom alerts and reports.

4
Creating Your Own Report Processor

In previous chapters, we've taken a look at some of the report processors that are shipped with Puppet and also some of the fantastic third-party plugins that have been developed to add new functionality. Now, it's time to show you how to go about making your own report plugins.

In this chapter, we're going to take a look at the following topics:

- Creating our first report processor
- Creating our own custom e-mail alerts
- Logging events into MySQL
- Raising issues with Atlassian JIRA

As with any Puppet plugin, our language of choice will be Ruby. You should be familiar with Ruby if you want to get the most out of this chapter; however, don't worry if you're not a Ruby guru; the examples use extremely basic code. If you need to brush up on your Ruby skills, then I highly recommend taking a look at *Learn Ruby the Hard Way, Zed A. Shaw*. Don't be put off by the title; it's both highly approachable and very effective in teaching you the basics of Ruby. It's available for free online or for purchase in e-book form at `http://ruby.learncodethehardway.org`.

The anatomy of a report processor

At its most basic, a Puppet report processor is a piece of Ruby code that is triggered every time a Puppet agent passes a report to the Puppet master. This piece of code is passed as a Ruby object that contains both the client report and metrics. Although the data is sent in a wire format, such as YAML or PSON, by the time a report processor is triggered, this data is turned into an object by Puppet. This code can simply provide reports, but we're not limited to that.

With a little imagination, we can use Puppet report processors for everything from alerts through to the orchestration of events. For instance, using a report processor and a suitable SMS provider would make it easy for Puppet to send you an SMS alert every time a run fails, or alternatively, using a report processor, you could analyze the data to reveal trends in your changes and update a change management console. The best way to think of a report processor is that it is a means to trigger actions on the event of a change, rather than strictly a reporting tool.

Puppet reports are written in plain old Ruby, and so you have access to the multitude of libraries available via the RubyGems repositories. This can make developing your plugins relatively simple, as half the time you will find that the heavy lifting has been done for you by some enterprising fellow who has already solved your problem and published his code in a gem. Good examples of this can be found if you need to interoperate with another product such as MySQL, Oracle, Salesforce, and so on. A brief search on the Internet will bring up three or four examples of libraries that will offer this functionality within a few lines of code. Not having to produce the plumbing of a solution will both save time and generally produce fewer bugs.

Creating a basic report processor

Let's take a look at an incredibly simple report processor example. In the event that a Puppet agent fails to run, the following code will take the incoming data and create a little text file with a short message detailing which host had the problem:

```
include puppet

Puppet::Reports::register_report(:myfirstreport) do
  desc "My very first report!"

  def process
    if self.status == 'failed'
      msg = "failed puppet run for #{self.host} #{self.status}
      File.open('./tmp/puppetpanic.txt', 'w') { | f |
        f.write(msg)}
    end
  end
end
```

Although this code is basic, it contains all of the components required for a report processor. The first line includes the only mandatory library required: the `Puppet` library. This gives us access to several important methods that allow us to register and describe our report processor, and finally, a method to allow us to process our data.

Downloading the example code

You can download the example code files for all Packt books you have purchased from your account at `http://www.packtpub.com`. If you purchased this book elsewhere, you can visit `http://www.packtpub.com/support` and register to have the files e-mailed directly to you.

Registering your report processor

The first method that every report processor must call is the `Puppet::Reports::register_report` method. This method can only take one argument, which is the name of the report processor. This name should be passed as a symbol and an alphanumeric title that starts with a letter (`:report3` would be fine, but `:3reports` would not be). Try to avoid using any other characters—although you can potentially use underscores, the documentation is rather discouragingly vague on how valid this is and could well cause issues.

Describing your report processor

After we've called the `Puppet::Reports::register_report` method, we then need to call the `desc` method. The `desc` method is used to provide some brief documentation for what the report processor does and allows the use of Markdown formatting in the string.

Processing your report

The last method that every report processor must include is the `process` method. The `process` method is where we actually take our Puppet data and process it, and to make working with the report data easier, you have access to the `.self` object within the `process` method. The `.self` object is a `Puppet::Transaction::Report` object and gives you access to the Puppet report data. For example, to extract the hostname of the reporting host, we can use the `self.host` object.

You can find the full details of what is contained in the `Puppet::Transaction::Report` object by visiting `http://docs.puppetlabs.com/puppet/latest/reference/format_report.html`.

Let's go through our small example in detail and look at what it's doing. First of all, we include the `Puppet` library to ensure that we have access to the required methods. We then register our report by calling the `Puppet::Reports::.register_report(:myfirstreport)` method and pass it the name of `myfirstreport`. Next, we add our `desc` method to tell users what this report is for. For the moment, we'll keep it simple and simply state its function. Finally, we have the `process` method, which is where we are going to place our code to process the report. For this example, we're going to keep it simple and simply check if the Puppet agent reported a successful run or not, and we do this by checking the Puppet status. This is described in the following code snippet:

```
if self.status == 'failed'
      msg = "failed puppet run for #{self.host}#{self.status}"
```

The transaction can produce one of three states: failed, changed, or unchanged. This is straightforward; a failed client run is any run that contains a resource that has a status of `failed`, a changed state is triggered when the client run contains a resource that has been given a status of `changed`, and the unchanged state occurs when a resource contains a value of `out_of_sync`; this generally happens if you run the Puppet client in noop (simulation) mode.

Finally, we actually do something with the data. In the case of this very simple application, we're going to place the warning into a plain text file in the `/tmp` directory. This is described in the following code snippet:

```
msg = "failed puppet run for #{self.host}"
File.open('/tmp/puppetpanic.txt', 'w') { | f | f.write(msg)}
```

As you can see, we're using basic string interpolation to take some of our report data and place it into the message. This is then written into a simple plain text file in the `/tmp` directory.

Values of the self.status object

The `self.status` object is something that you are going to use again and again when constructing your own report processors. The `self.status` object value allows you to filter Puppet reports, based on the status that the Puppet agent reported after attempting to apply the catalog. The following values are available:

- `skipped`: A skipped resource essentially means that Puppet evaluated the resource and decided for one reason or another that it was not going to apply the requested change. The most common reason for skipped resources is that there is a failed resource somewhere else in the transaction that this change depends on. Other reasons could include that a resource belongs to one tag while you're applying a different tag, or it may be an entirely virtual resource.

- `failed`: A resource is marked as failed when the Puppet client is unable to apply a change to that resource. This can simply mean that it could not change a file, instantiate a directory, or install a package.
- `failed_to_restart`: This particular status only applies to service resource objects and is flagged anytime that Puppet tries to restart a service and fails.
- `restarted`: This is another service-oriented status and is the inverse to the `failed_to_restart` status. Essentially, a resource is flagged as this when it is a service that has been successfully restarted.
- `changed`: This is one of the most common status types that you will see in Puppet, and it tells you that this particular resource has been changed during the course of the Puppet catalog's application.
- `out_of_sync`: This should only occur when the Puppet run is triggered in simulation mode (noop). This is a resource that would be changed if the Puppet catalog was applied.

That's all that is required for a working Puppet report processor. This tiny chunk of code will happily parse incoming reports, evaluate, and act on them. Of course, this is a fairly useless report in its current form, but it gives us a good idea of what we can do. Let's take a look at something a little more solid, shall we?

Alerting with e-mail and Puppet

The tagmail report processor is a useful plugin, but it has its limitations. As pointed out in its name, it can only deal with tags and nothing else. Sometimes, that's not quite what you want, so it's useful to see how simple it is to produce an e-mail alert that you can tailor to your requirements. In our case, we're going to create a simple e-mail alert that will be sent every time a Puppet agent makes a change.

This may seem a little odd; after all, what's Puppet for if not to enact changes? There are some environments, however, where changes are a highly sensitive matter. Change can, and should, be easy in certain environments, and this is particularly true of many web applications. The reverse can also be true in cases where you are either dealing with a heavily audited environment, such as a financial trading system, or a system that deals with highly sensitive and business-critical systems, such as an API that feeds phone handsets or set top boxes. In these cases, changes need to be very strictly controlled, and any change that is made by accident needs to be both alerted and dealt with swiftly.

The first task we need to take care of is the creation of our project. We're going to follow the best practice set out in the previous chapter and create this in the form of a Puppet module. Rather than create the directory layouts by hand, I'm going to use the Puppet module creation utility included with Puppet. This can be done using the following command:

```
puppet module generate <username>-<modulename>
```

The username is your Puppet Forge username. If you haven't signed up for one, don't worry; you can add any text you like here for the moment. Once we have created our module, the next thing to do is to create the file that will contain our code. Since it is a report plugin, it should be created in the following location:

```
{module}
    └── lib
          └── puppet
                  └──reports
                          └── {reportname}
```

You'll need to create some of the directory structure by hand as the Puppet module's `generate` command doesn't include the `lib` directory or subdirectories by default.

Once you've created your file structure, you're ready to code. Go ahead and create a new file called `changealert.rb` in the `lib` directory and add the following first part of the code to it:

```
require 'puppet'
begin
require 'mail'
rescueLoadError
Puppet.info 'This report requires the mail gem to run'
end
```

Note the error handling around the `mail` gem. This is good practice if you're planning on distributing your report as it ensures that if there is a missing gem, it is handled gracefully and gives the user some sort of clue as to why it may not have run correctly. Nothing is more irritating than having to wade through someone else's code to find the obscure library they forgot to mention in the `readme.txt` file. Good coding habits like this one can go a long way if you start releasing your code on GitHub or Puppet Forge, and it will help people both use your module and contribute towards it.

As in the previous example, we need to go ahead and declare our new report. We're also going to declare our `process` function and load our configuration.

If your report processor requires any kind of configuration, then make sure that this is loaded from an external configuration file; and, as an absolute best practice, store it in the Puppet configuration directory. This means that your code is easily redistributable, and more importantly, it is obviously configurable by anyone who installs it.

Consider the following code:

```
Puppet::Reports.register_report(:changealert) do
    configfile =
      File.join([File.dirname(Puppet.settings[:config]),
      'changealert.yaml'])
    raise(Puppet::ParseError, "auditlert configfile not readable")
      unless File.exist?(configfile)
    config = YAML.load_file(configfile)
```

As you can see, we're loading the configuration for this report processor from a `.yaml` file, but before we can load it, there are a few tasks we need to carry out first. To start with, we need to find out where the configuration file is held. This is not as straightforward as you may think; for starters, Puppet Open Source and Puppet Enterprise hold configuration files in different locations (`/etc/puppet` and `/etc/puppetmaster`, respectively). To add to this, you can relocate the configuration directory into an arbitrary location of your choice, and you quickly realize that it would be a seriously bad idea to hardcode the path. Instead, we can ask Puppet where the configuration directory is. To do this, we call the `class` method settings from the Puppet class and feed it into the `configfile` variable. Using these kinds of techniques guarantees that if you publish your work, it will be usable for the widest array of users.

The next thing that we need to do is actually check if the configuration file is present, and if not, raise an error. Using the `Puppet::ParseError` object, we are able to raise an error to the Parser. This means that if there is an issue, it will be immediately visible in the Puppet log, and especially visible if we are running the Puppet agent in interactive mode. Once we have checked that the file is present, we then use the `YAML` class to load the file and place its contents into a new object called `config`. Once loaded into this object, the file can then be accessed as a Ruby hash. For instance, to find out the SMTP address of the mail server, we could use the `config['smtp_address']` command to return a string that contains the configuration item.

That's the basic framework taken care of. We're going to add some logic at this point to ensure that we only receive reports for Puppet agent runs that result in the changed state rather than in the unchanged and failed states. This is described in the following code snippet:

```
If self.status == 'changed'
      subject = "Host #{self.host} Change alert"
      output = []
```

Once we've ascertained that this particular run is of interest to us, we set up a string variable that will contain our e-mail header and create an empty array to hold subsequent data.

This particular plugin is designed to simply let someone know if something has changed, so we don't really need to send the user the entire output of the Puppet report. If you have a critical system that's just received an update that you weren't expecting, you are probably not interested in how long it took to apply, but rather in what change has been applied and when it was applied. This kind of alert is much better short and pithy. To accomplish this, we're going to list the following details in the e-mail:

- The resources that have changed
- The type of resource
- The type of property that has changed
- The value it was changed to
- The time when it was changed

This gives our user plenty of information to go on, without overloading them with lots of irrelevant nonsense. The following code describes our e-mail alert:

```
output << "The Following resources have changed:\n"
    begin
      self.resource_statuses.each do
        |theresource,resource_status|
        if resource_status.change_count > 0
          output << "Resource: #{resource_status.title}"
          output << "Type: #{resource_status.resource_type}"
            begin resource_status.events.each do |event|
              output << "Property: #{event.property}"
              output << "Value: #{event.desired_value}"
              output << "Status: #{event.status}"
              output << "Time: #{event.time}"
```

```
                    end
                  end
              end
            end
          end
```

The first thing that this piece of code does is output a little header letting us know what this report is about—it's always nice when it's 2 A.M. and you're wading through e-mails because you've been woken up by the support phone. I'm using the Ruby string concatenation syntax to build up our report in a variable called `output`; notice the `\n` at the end of that line? It's to ensure that we have a clean line break between the header and the rest of the report.

Next, we read the array that contains the reported resources, the `resource_status` property, and use a Ruby block to iterate through each resource and check its `change_count` property. If it's greater than zero, then we know that some form of change has taken place and we have to examine it further.

> Over time, several items in the `Puppet::Resource::Status` object are marked as deprecated. The Puppet report format is now in its 4th version as of the time of writing and is evolving as new features are added and old ones removed. It's worth keeping an eye on the release notes when a new version is released to ensure that your report plugins continue to work as expected.

Once we find a changed resource, we then take the values from the `resource_status.title` and `resource_status.resource_type` properties and concatenate them into our output variable. This data will allow the report recipient to figure out what resource has changed and what type of resource it is.

Now that we've found a resource of interest, we start a new loop and iterate inside the event array to find the details of the change itself. The `Puppet::Transaction::Event` object holds a wealth of information, and from it, you can derive information such as when a change took place, the previous value of the resource, the desired value, and so on. When you find yourself asking, "What's happened on this node?", then it's the `Puppet::Transaction::Event` object that holds the answer to this question.

> You can find a complete list of the fields available in the `Puppet::Transaction::Event` object at `http://docs.puppetlabs.com/puppet/3/reference/format_report.html#puppettransactionevent-1`.

For the moment, we're going to show the user the `Property`, `Value`, `Status`, and `Time` properties; this should be plenty to tip off our sleepy on-call person as to what has changed, when it has changed, and to what it has changed. This should be plenty of information to start figuring out what caused this particular resource to change.

At this point, we have gathered our data, and it is time to send it on its way. To send the data, this particular report processor is going to use an SMTP mail server. Pretty much every company has access to an SMTP server, so it's a fairly safe route to take when it comes to sending data. We've already started to construct the e-mail that will be sent to our user; the code that we've already explored has constructed the body of the message. Now, we simply need to add in some further details and then use the `mail` library to send it. The values that we are going to use have already been included in our configuration file, and we have already decanted these values into a hash that is ready to be accessed. This is described in the following code snippet:

```
body = output.join("\n")

      Mail.defaults do
        delivery_method :smtp, {
            :address => config['smtp_server'],
            :port => config['port'],
            :domain => config['smtp_domain'],
            :user_name => config['smtp_username'],
            :password => config['smtp_password'],
            :authentication => 'login',
            :enable_starttls_auto => false
        }

      end

      Mail.deliver do
        toto_address
        fromfrom_address
        subject subject
        body body
      end
    end
  end
end
```

In the preceding code, we instantiate a `Mail` object and use its `defaults` method to supply it a list of settings to send to our mail. In this case, I've elected to use SMTP, so we need to provide a username and password to authenticate our plugin. We also need to give it the address of the SMTP server, which TCP port it needs to send the data to, and finally, which login mechanism we're using. Although I'm using an SMTP server, you could just as easily use Exim, Sendmail, or a local delivery: the `Mail` gem supports all of them. Once configured, sending the e-mail is simple; we just need to call the `Mail.deliver` function and let it know where to send it to, who it's from, and then give it the header and body we've created.

That's all of the code we need to make this work; however, there is still one last piece left, and that's the configuration file. The configuration file is a simple YAML document named `changealert.yaml` that needs to be placed inside the root of the Puppet master configuration file. Inside it are all of the details required to configure our plugin, and it should look something like the following:

```
from_address: 'alerts@fictionalco.com'
to_address: 'devops@fictionalco.com'
smtp_server: 'mailserver@fictionalco.com'
smtp_domain: 'fictionalco.com'
smtp_username: 'alertuser'
smtp_password: 'b3ty0uc@ntgu355m3'
```

Now that we have the configuration file, we're ready to go; when we're ready, we'll install the change alert module, add it to the reports configuration in the Puppet master, and trigger a Puppet agent. If all has gone well, we should receive a message via e-mail that looks a little like the following:

```
The Following resources have changed:

Resource: git
Type: Package
Property: ensure
Value: present
Status: success
Time: 2014-01-15 07:52:03 +0000
```

Voila! Our very own custom e-mail alert with very little code.

The techniques used here are the core part of any report processor, and as you can see, the bulk of the code actually deals with sending the e-mail rather than extracting the data. Puppet has made accessing the data very easy indeed, leaving you free to concentrate on what you want to do with it. In almost every report processor, you will find that there is more code that deals with processing the data than extracting it.

If you find that your report plugin is turning into an especially complex piece of code, then you may want to consider moving it to an external report handler and either feed the data via the HTTP plugin or read the reports produced by the store plugin. A report processor is fired each and every time a report configured client runs Puppet, and if your plugin is taking a fair chunk of time and resources to process the data, then you are soon going to feel the pain in the performance of your Puppet infrastructure.

Managing your report processor configuration with Puppet

The change alert report processor is pretty cool, and by packaging it inside a Puppet module, we've made it easy to be distributed; however, we have left the user to create a configuration file to make it work. This is not necessarily a bad thing, and as long as we have a well-documented example of the configuration in the `Readme.txt` file, then most users should be more or less OK. It is not really in keeping with Puppet though; we can make end users' lives a little easier by giving them the option to have Puppet manage the report processor configuration for them. We already have a Puppet module with an `init.pp` file, and we can easily leverage this and a Puppet template to create the configuration file. From the perspective of the Puppet code, this is very simple and essentially comprises three components: a parameterized Puppet class, file resource, and file template. Let's start with the Puppet class and file resource. They are described in the following code snippet:

```
class changealert (
  $from_address,
  $to_address,
  $smtp_server,
  $smtp_domain,
  $smtp_username,
  $smtp_password
  ) {
  file {"${settings::confdir}/changealert.yaml":
    owner    => 'puppet',
    group    => 'puppet',
    mode     => '0644',
```

```
        content => template('changealert/changealert.erb'),
    }
}
```

If you are reasonably familiar with Puppet, then this code should be straightforward. In the first line, we declare a new Puppet class named `changealert`; we then add the six parameters that are required for our template. Note that I'm not giving any default values to the parameters, and this is quite deliberate; none of the parameters are optional, so we want this manifest to fail early and fail fast.

After we have set up our class, we then declare a file resource for the `changealert.yaml` file. I'm using some built-in Puppet variables to find out where the configuration directory is and ensuring that the file is created there. I'm also ensuring that the Puppet user and group own the file and setting sensible file permissions. Finally, I'm declaring that the content is derived from a template, which I'm sourcing from the module itself. The template is a simple one and takes our parameters and places them into the file. This is described in the following code snippet:

```
from_address: <%= @from_address %>
to_address: <%= @to_address %>
smtp_server: <%= @smtp_server %>
smtp_domain: <%= @smtp_domain %>
smtp_username: <%= @smtp_username %>
smtp_password: <%= @smtp_password %>
```

Our end user now has the choice to configure the change alert report by simply declaring the class on any Puppet master they are managing using Puppet. An example of doing this using a manifest would look something like the following:

```
node 'puppet.example.com' {
  class {'changealert':
    from_address  => 'michael@stunthamster.com',
    to_address    => 'puppet@exampleco.com,
    smtp_server   => 'smtp.exampleco.com',
    smtp_domain   => 'exampleco.com',
    smtp_username => 'smtpuser@exampleco.com,
    smtp_password => 'weakpassword'
  }
}
```

If we did it using Hiera, it would look something like the following:

```
classes: changealert
changealert::from_address: puppet@exampleco.com
changealert::to_address: puppet@exampleco.com
```

```
changealert::smtp_server: smtp.exampleco.com
changealert::smtp_domain: exampleco.com
changealert::smtp_username: smtpuser@exampleco.com
changealert::smtp_password: weakpassword
```

Of course, we still leave the user with the option of configuring the report processor in the way they choose; simply installing the module will ensure that the report processor is installed, and if the user does not declare the Puppet class to manage the configuration file, then Puppet will not attempt to manage it.

Monitoring changes and alerting with Puppet

Our change alert report processor is pretty useful and will inform us when something we've managed has been changed. That's excellent, but there are times when we want to monitor resources that are not necessarily something we also want to manage. A good example is the `passwd` file in the `/etc` directory. We will never manage this file directly with Puppet; we have the user and group resource types to do that, but we may still want to know when something has changed it. Luckily, we can do this using the somewhat overlooked audit option within a resource.

Auditing was introduced in Puppet 2.6.0 and allows you to specify a nonmanaged resource within a Puppet manifest. The `audit` metaparameter tells Puppet that although you do not want to manage the resource, you'd still like it to make note of its values and log when it changes. Take a look at the following example Puppet code:

```
file { '/etc/passwd':
audit => [ owner, group, mode ],
}
```

From now on, whenever the `/etc/passwd` file's owner, group, or permissions are changed, Puppet will make note of the previous value, the time at which it was changed, and the value it was changed to. You don't need to be selective either; you can ask Puppet to audit everything it possibly can about a resource. This is described in the following code snippet:

```
file { '/etc/hosts':
audit => all,
}
```

Now, if anything changes on that file, from the owner to the content and anything in between, the Puppet agent will note it down in its report.

This is a fantastically powerful tool when combined with Puppet reporting and alerting. You can use it for anything from a basic **Intrusion Detection System (IDS)** to a software auditing tool for licensing and anything in between. If you're running your Puppet clients on a regular basis, such as in daemonized mode, then you can be sure of receiving the alert in good time (30 minutes if you're using the default interval). Of course, for this we need a report processor; luckily, it won't take much to wrangle the change alert plugin into a shiny new audit alert plugin.

An audited resource is a little different from a normal one from the reporting perspective. When a Puppet run encounters a change in an audited resource, it is noted down as an event in the `Puppet::Transaction::Event` object, the same as a normal event, but with the value of the audited attribute set to `true`. This is great news as it means that we have very little work to do to transform our change alert processor into an audit alert processor.

As you can see, the bulk of the code remains the same, mostly made up of the tedious business of constructing and sending the e-mail object. Instead of processing the data as we did in the previous example, this time we are going to do it as follows:

```
begin
      self.resource_statuses.each do |theresource,
        resource_status|
        begin
          resource_status.events.each do |event|
            if event.audited then
              output << resource_status.title
              output << "Audited #{event.audited}"
              output << "Property: #{event.property}"
              self.logs.each do |log|
                if log.source.include? resource_status.title
                  output << log.message
                end
              end
              output << "Status: #{event.status}"
              output << "Time: #{event.time}"
              send_report = true
            end
          end
        end
      end
end
```

This is a fairly simple piece of code and should be recognizable from our previous plugin. It's undertaking the same basic journey; enable the resources and then traverse the events array. The difference this time is that we have a very simple piece of logic that looks out for the audited flag within the resources, and if it's set to `true`, iterates through the matching events to find the details of the change. Once we have gathered the data, we then set a flag to ensure that an e-mail is sent.

Again, this is a simple report but is a really neat way to use the audit flag. Using this, you can keep an eye on files, packages, users, and other resources without needing to directly manage them. You are not limited to just the standard resources; any custom resource you've developed should also be able to make use of this, and the type of alert can be anything. If you don't like e-mail, then it would be relatively easy to have this processor send you alerts via SMS, Twitter, or any other method you can trigger via Ruby.

Logging with MySQL

If there is one technology that you're almost guaranteed to find in most companies, it is SQL. One of the enormous advantages of Puppet is that it can make change activities hugely transparent, and this is an enormously rich piece of data that can complement existing reports exceptionally well. For instance, your organization may already have reports noting how many transactions have taken place over a certain time period, and when looking at any sudden gains or losses to the average, it's fantastic to be able to add in change activity. Suddenly, you will see that the drop in user transactions coincides with the web server that is pushing out a new version of `nginx`, or the jump in sales happened just after the new version of the sales application was pushed by Puppet.

This is valuable data, but to get the most out of it, it needs to be available to the people who construct these reports. For many organizations, this means that the data will be held in a SQL database; not only is it common in terms of skill base and technology, it's almost guaranteed that any reporting tool worth its salt will be able to work with it.

Fortunately, it's simple to get Puppet to store its reports in SQL, and most of what we have learned about creating our simple alerts is just as applicable to exporting data. As with most report processors, we're going to use a library to do the heavy lifting, which will leave us free to concentrate on the interesting bits.

The first thing that we should do is go ahead and install the required library to allow Ruby to work with MySQL. This gem makes use of native extensions and so will need to have some development libraries installed. To install the packages, perform the following steps:

1. Install the MySQL Ruby library.

   On Debian-based distributions, it's installed using the following command:

   ```
   sudo apt-get install libmysql-ruby libmysqlclient-dev
   ```

   On RedHat-based distributions, it's installed using the following command:

   ```
   sudo yum install mysql-devel
   ```

2. Install the `sequel` library using the following command:

   ```
   sudo gem install sequel
   ```

Why not MySQL2?

The sequel gem is a little more powerful than the common MySQL2 gem and is a lightweight **Object-relational Mapping** (**ORM**) tool; this offers the ability to abstract ourselves away from using SQL and instead allows us to concentrate on code. When used as an ORM, it also ensures that any strings are treated as SQL strings and, therefore, makes us much less susceptible to SQL injection attacks.

Now that we've installed our prerequisites for the code, we need somewhere to put the data, which means we need to get our hands dirty with MySQL. I'm going to go ahead and assume that you have MySQL installed; if not, it's relatively easy using the package manager of your distribution. Once it's installed, you can run the log into MySQL and run the following SQL query:

```
CREATE DATABASE puppet_stats;
```

This straightforward query will create an empty database named `puppet_stats`, but before we set up our tables, let's also go ahead and create a user. From a security perspective, it's a bad idea to use the root user, so let's go ahead and create a user specifically for this report processor inside MySQL. This can be done using the following SQL query:

```
CREATE USER 'puppetreporting'@'localhost' IDENTIFIED BY
  'changeme';
GRANT ALL ON puppet_stats.* TO 'puppetreporting'@'localhost';
```

We've now got somewhere to store the data and got a database as well, so the next thing we need to do is create the first table. This can be done as follows:

```
USE puppet_stats;

CREATE TABLE reports (
transaction_uuid VARCHAR(50),
Host TEXT,
Date DATE,
Time TIME,
Kind TEXT,
Report_format INTEGER,
Puppet_version TEXT,
Environment TEXT,
Status TEXT,
PRIMARY KEY (transaction_uuid));
```

This will create a table to store our first piece of data: the contents of the `puppet::transaction::report` object. We will add the following fields into our table:

- UUID
- The date of the Puppet run
- The time of the Puppet run
- The kind of run (inspect run, agent run, and so on)
- The version of the report format
- The Puppet agent version
- The environment it was run in
- The status of the Puppet run

Finally, we're going to set the primary key of the table to the **Universally Unique Identifier** (**UUID**). The UUID is a completely unique identifier that Puppet creates with each and every run, so it's perfect to key the table with. In fact, when we need to split the Puppet data into relational datasets, we can use the UUID to query the data.

If you're a little rusty on your database knowledge, then you can brush up by visiting `http://dev.mysql.com/doc/`. This will take you through the basics that you'll need to follow this code.

Now that we have our table set up, we can go ahead and create a report to fill it. The first task is to include the libraries that we require for this report processor to function. This is described in the following code snippet:

```
require 'puppet'
require 'logger'
require 'yaml'
require 'date'

begin
  require 'sequel'
rescue LoadError
  Puppet.info 'This report requires the sequel gem to run'
end
```

We are already familiar with the `puppet` library, but we have some new libraries this time round. First of all, we have included the `logger` library, a library that is shipped with Ruby. The `logger` library allows you to emit simple log messages from your application to the file of your choosing. Like most log utilities, it will allow us to set different reporting levels, from `FATAL` (which means, "Good Lord, my program has just crashed!") through to `DEBUG` ("Good grief! My program has just done something!"). Using these log levels, you are able to make your report processor much more verbose if it encounters an error.

Notice how the Puppet `date`, `yaml`, and `logger require` statements are not wrapped in our usual logic to check for their presence? That's because these are default libraries shipped with Ruby so you can be pretty certain that the end user is going to have them, whereas the `sequel` library may have been missed out.

That takes care of the setup of the report processor. Next up, we have our process function. Consider the following code snippet:

```
@log = Logger.new('/var/log/puppet/puppetreport.log')

    configfile =
      File.join([File.dirname(Puppet.settings[:config]),
     'mysqlreport.yaml'])
    raise(Puppet::ParseError, "mysqlreport configfile not
      readable") unless File.exist?(configfile)
    config = YAML.load_file(configfile)

    db = Sequel.connect(:adapter => 'mysql',
                        :user => config['mysqlusername'],
```

```
                                    :host => config['mysqlserver'],
                                    :database => 'puppet_stats',
                                    :password=>config['mysqlpassword'])
        reports = db.from(:reports)

        puppet_time_stamp = DateTime.parse("#{self.time}")
```

As you can see, we have the usual class declaration with the report name and process function. The next line specifies the location of our logfile; if you're on a Linux system, then the `/var/log/puppet` directory is always a good bet. Make sure that whatever location you choose has both read and write access from your Puppet user, as that is the user executing the code.

Next, we define our configuration file location and load it, again checking that it is present and loading it into our `config` variable. Our configuration file contains the server name of our MySQL server, the username we're going to use, and finally, the password. It should look like the following:

```
mysqlserver: mysql@fictionalco.com
mysqlusername: puppetreporting
mysqlpassword: Dontuseweakpasswords
```

Again, we can use the same technique that we used in the change alert and audit alert examples to define this configuration for us using Puppet. In this case, the `init.pp` file would look like the following:

```
class mysqlreport (
  $mysql_server,
  $mysql_username,
  $mysql_password
) {

  file {"${settings::confdir}/mysqlreport.yaml":
    owner   => 'puppet',
    group   => 'puppet',
    mode    => '0644',
    content => template('mysqlreport/mysqlreport.erb'),
  }
}
```

Now that we have our configuration items, we can set up our connection to the MySQL database using the `sequel` library. As you can see, we're using string interpolation to insert the contents of our configuration file into the connection string. The connection string is made up of the server name, username, password, and the database that we wish to connect to. We've been supplied the first three parts by the user, and we've hardcoded the database name so that it matches our preceding SQL scripts. We pass this information into a new variable called `db`, which we use in the next line to create a new object called `reports`. We then instantiate this object by supplying our database connection and the table we want to map to.

Now that we have set up our database connection, we can start to make use of the `date` library. The Puppet report expresses its timestamp in a date-time format, that is, in a combined field made up of both the time and the date; this is perfectly fine and is supported by the MySQL `DATETIME` field format. However, I've found that almost every time I've had to place data into SQL, the requirements have been to have a separate date and time field to ease reporting. Fortunately, with Ruby, this is relatively easy with the `date` library. As you can see, we take the contents of the `self.time` function and run it through the `DateTime.parse` function. The output is then placed into a variable called `puppet_time_stamp`; this then allows us to split the date and time into two subsequent fields using the `strftime` function.

> To find out more about the `strftime` function, you can check the Ruby documentation at `http://www.ruby-doc.org/core-2.1.0/Time.html`.

Now that we've set up our database connection and arranged the date format to our satisfaction, we're ready to start adding data. Consider the following code snippet:

```
reports.insert(
        :transaction_uuid => self.transaction_uuid,
        :Host => self.host,
        :Date => puppet_time_stamp.strftime('%Y-%m-%d'),
        :Time => puppet_time_stamp.strftime('%H:%M:%S'),
        :Kind => self.kind,
        :Report_format => self.report_format,
        :Puppet_version => self.puppet_version,
        :Environment => self.environment,
```

```
            :Status => self.status
          )

        rescue => err
          @log.fatal('Caught exception; exiting')
          @log.fatal(err)
        end

      end

    end
```

Using the `sequel` library as an ORM, we can easily insert data into our table without needing to use SQL code. This has two advantages; firstly, it's much more readable, and secondly, the `sequel` library converts any strings you insert into a properly formatted SQL string. This ensures that you are not at risk of a SQL injection attack.

> A SQL injection is essentially when someone uses an input into SQL to add in their own code. This can happen anytime you process data that has not originated from your code, such as a text input field. In our case, it's derived from Puppet data, but a cunning attacker could potentially use this if they sent a specially crafted Puppet report. A humorous example of what a SQL injection is can be found in the XKCD webcomic at `http://xkcd.com/327/`.

To insert the data, we call the `insert` function from our `reports` object. This function takes a comma-separated list of key value pairs, with each pair made up of the column and the value you want to insert. In our case, we simply insert the data straight from Puppet's `puppet::Transaction::Report` object, with the exception of the time and date values. In this case, we use the `strftime` method to split a singular date stamp into a separate date and time object before inserting it.

The final two lines of the preceding code, once again, use the `logger` library to help us diagnose issues. You'll find that if your SQL code fails for some reason—say, if your MySQL server is down or you've ended up with some strange characters in your query—then you're going to have a hard time diagnosing the issue. By default, the Puppet master will log a very small piece of data, simply noting in the default Puppet log that it encountered a fault while running the Puppet processor. This could lead to quite a long bout of head scratching as you try to figure out why. The `rescue` directive will tell Ruby to catch any error that is generated and allow us to process the resulting data. In our case, we log a fatal error, log the error message to our log, and exit the report processor. It's worth noting that this will not affect the Puppet master; it will carry on serving Puppet requests even if a report processor has exited with an error.

Add your new report processor to the Puppet master in the usual way, then restart and watch your data start to appear in MySQL. If everything went right, you should be able to perform a simple select query to see your data as shown in the following screenshot:

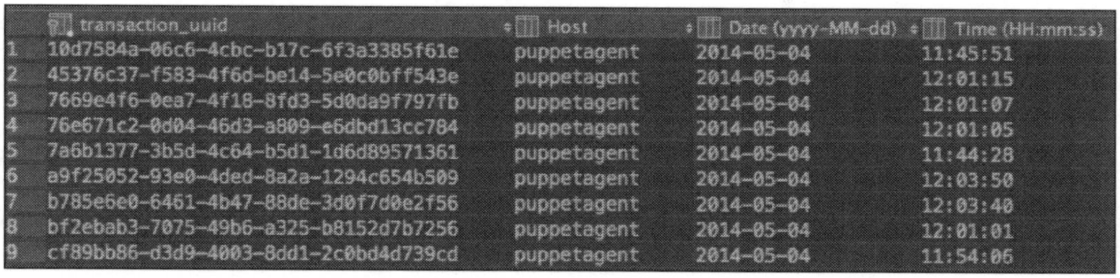

	transaction_uuid	Host	Date (yyyy-MM-dd)	Time (HH:mm:ss)
1	10d7584a-06c6-4cbc-b17c-6f3a3385f61e	puppetagent	2014-05-04	11:45:51
2	45376c37-f583-4f6d-be14-5e0c0bff543e	puppetagent	2014-05-04	12:01:15
3	7669e4f6-0ea7-4f18-8fd3-5d0da9f797fb	puppetagent	2014-05-04	12:01:07
4	76e671c2-0d04-46d3-a809-e6dbd13cc784	puppetagent	2014-05-04	12:01:05
5	7a6b1377-3b5d-4c64-b5d1-1d6d89571361	puppetagent	2014-05-04	11:44:28
6	a9f25052-93e0-4ded-8a2a-1294c654b509	puppetagent	2014-05-04	12:03:50
7	b785e6e0-6461-4b47-88de-3d0f7d0e2f56	puppetagent	2014-05-04	12:03:40
8	bf2ebab3-7075-49b6-a325-b8152d7b7256	puppetagent	2014-05-04	12:01:01
9	cf89bb86-d3d9-4003-8dd1-2c0bd4d739cd	puppetagent	2014-05-04	11:54:06

The trouble is that this isn't really of much use to us; we know that a Puppet run has taken place, and what its status was, but we have very little detail otherwise. Let's go ahead and add some detail in the form of Puppet metrics.

Adding metrics and events to MySQL

Metrics can give you a good feel of how your Puppet-managed infrastructure is performing and how rapidly your configuration items are changing. Combined with the Puppet report, the metrics and events can add a wealth of data to your reports. This is where MySQL can shine, as it gives you several different ways to represent this information and offers you the chance to use SQL to create your own reports. As the data will be available in one place, there is no need to crawl through multiple files to build up historical data or join data using the `JOIN` statement.

The Puppet metrics are carried inside the Puppet transaction report and are encapsulated within the `Puppet::Util::Metric` object. The metric data is split up between resources, events, and changes, and each category has its own timings for its various elements. For instance, within the resources category, we are able to see metrics for how many resources are in the failed, out of sync, or changed state. Like almost all the Puppet report data, this is expressed in the form of arrays, with each category containing an array of metrics.

Adding metrics to our existing MySQL report processor is fairly easy, and we can easily link the data using the UUID that we are already inserting. We could potentially place this data alongside our existing data, but this would lead to a fair chunk of data duplication, huge rows of data, and, quite probably, an angry DBA at your doorstep. It's far better to start splitting the data out, or in the lingo of DBAs, "normalize the data".

Normalizing the Puppet report is easy as it's pretty much already been done for you. The data in the `Puppet::Util::Metric` object is easily mapped into a table and column relationship. In this case, we're going to take the entirety of the `Puppet::Util::Metric` object and place it into a row inside a new table within our database. Let's start by creating the table within MySQL using the following SQL query:

```
CREATE TABLE metrics (
transaction_uuid VARCHAR(50),
res_changed INT,
res_failed INT,
res_failed_restart INT,
res_out_sync INT,
res_restarted INT,
res_scheduled INT,
res_skipped INT,
res_total INT,
time_conf_ret FLOAT,
time_file FLOAT,
time_filebucket FLOAT,
time_package FLOAT,
time_schedule FLOAT,
time_total INT,
changes_total INT,
events_failure INT,
events_success INT,
events_total INT,
PRIMARY KEY (transaction_uuid))
```

Now that we have our metrics table, let's go ahead and insert the new code to iterate and insert the metrics. This goes just underneath our first SQL statement and is made up of two parts. Firstly, we need to iterate through the metrics data and place it into an array of key pairs that we can then easily access. This is described in the following code snippet:

```
        reports.insert(
            :transaction_uuid => self.transaction_uuid,
            :Host => self.host,
            :Date => puppet_time_stamp.strftime('%Y-%m-%d'),
            :Time => puppet_time_stamp.strftime('%H:%M:%S'),
            :Kind => self.kind,
            :Report_format => self.report_format,
            :Puppet_version => self.puppet_version,
            :Environment => self.environment,
```

```
            :Status => self.status
        )

metric_vals = {}

        self.metrics.each { |metric, data|
          data.values.each { |val|
            name = "#{val[1]} #{metric}"
            value = val[2]
            metric_vals[name] = value
          }
        }
```

Firstly, we create an empty array in which to hold our metrics, and then we iterate through the `self.metrics` array and pull out each of the categories. For each category, we then gather its statistics. Once we have the metric and its value, we insert it into our `metric_vals` array and then start the loop again.

Once we have all our values, we then need to insert it into our metrics tables. Once again, we use the `sequel` library to assign our table, this time to a variable called `metrics`. Then, we call the `insert` method and pass it the comma-separated list of key values that we gathered from the Puppet metrics. One thing to note is that we once again insert the UUID, and this allows us to use a `JOIN` query within SQL to tie our metrics and report table together. This is described in the following code:

```
metrics = db.from(:metrics)
      metrics.insert(
          :transaction_uuid => self.transaction_uuid,
          :res_changed => metric_vals['Changed resources'],
          :res_failed => metric_vals['Failed resources'],
          :res_failed_restart => metric_vals['Failed to restart
            resources'],
          :res_out_sync => metric_vals['Out of sync resources'],
          :res_restarted => metric_vals['Restarted resources'],
          :res_scheduled => metric_vals['Scheduled resources'],
          :res_skipped => metric_vals['Skipped resources'],
          :res_total => metric_vals['Total resources'],
          :time_conf_ret => metric_vals['Config retrieval time'],
          :time_file => metric_vals['File time'],
          :time_filebucket => metric_vals['Filebucket time'],
          :time_package => metric_vals['Package time'],
          :time_schedule => metric_vals['Schedule time'],
          :time_total => metric_vals['Total time'],
          :changes_total => metric_vals['Total changes'],
```

```
            :events_failure => metric_vals['Failure events'],
            :events_success => metric_vals['Success events'],
            :events_total => metric_vals['Total events']
      )

    rescue => err
      @log.fatal('Caught exception; exiting')
      @log.fatal(err)
    end
```

Now, if you run your Puppet agents, you should find that additional data has been created in your metrics table. If you query it, you should find that your data looks a little something like the following screenshot:

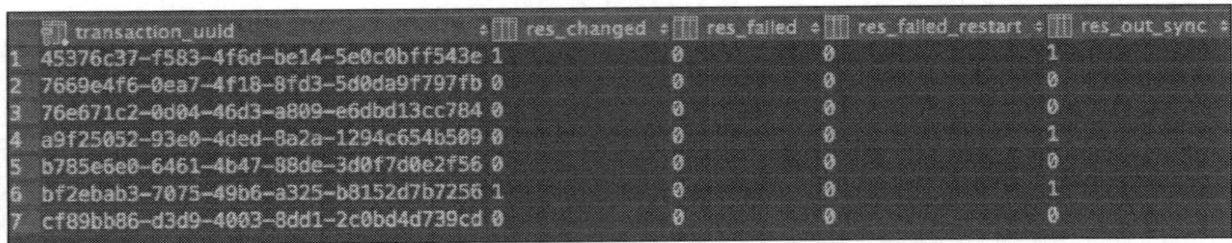

	transaction_uuid	res_changed	res_failed	res_failed_restart	res_out_sync
1	45376c37-f583-4f6d-be14-5e0c0bff543e	1	0	0	1
2	7669e4f6-0ea7-4f18-8fd3-5d0da9f797fb	0	0	0	0
3	76e671c2-0d04-46d3-a809-e6dbd13cc784	0	0	0	0
4	a9f25052-93e0-4ded-8a2a-1294c654b509	0	0	0	1
5	b785e6e0-6461-4b47-88de-3d0f7d0e2f56	0	0	0	0
6	bf2ebab3-7075-49b6-a325-b8152d7b7256	1	0	0	1
7	cf89bb86-d3d9-4003-8dd1-2c0bd4d739cd	0	0	0	0

That about wraps it up for the MySQL report processor. You have seen how to take the data that Puppet produces and feed it into a platform like MySQL. By exporting your data, you're making it more accessible to other users and tools, and you'll be surprised at what other people can come up with when they are handed this type of data. I've seen some fantastic business dashboards that have mashed up Puppet data with server statistics and throughput. The basic rule of thumb when it comes to Puppet data is that if someone asks, "Can I get the data in the format I need?", the answer, invariably, is yes.

Raising issues with JIRA

There's one final example we're going to look at before I leave you to experiment on your own, and that's how to automatically raise issues with **Atlassian JIRA**. This is worthwhile on two fronts: firstly, JIRA is a fantastic tool for bug and issue tracking, and secondly, it will give you a sense of how to integrate Puppet with third-party tools.

Atlassian JIRA has been around since 2002, and in this time, has become one of the most popular forms of issue-tracking software on the market, in use by an estimated 25,000 organizations. Part of the appeal of JIRA is that it is a web-based product, and it is very easy to install and maintain. Recently, Atlassian has offered JIRA to its users in the form of a Software as a Service package, which has lowered the barrier to entry for running JIRA even further. One of the things that set JIRA apart fairly early on was its excellent API, as it allowed people to create products and services that would easily be able to integrate with JIRA with minimal effort.

Issue tracking is a natural fit for a Puppet report plugin. There are times when you don't want to receive an e-mail when there is a problem with a Puppet run, but by the same token, you also want to make a record of the issue so that you can go back and solve it later. Using JIRA and a suitable report processor, you will be able to have Puppet quietly raise an issue if it encounters a problem so that developers can track and fix the issue.

You might be surprised to find that this is the simplest example yet. Unlike SQL servers and e-mails, we have no need to build up relatively complex data structures; it can all be dealt by a single call to the JIRA API. A big part of the brevity of the code is that we are using a Ruby library that bundles the JIRA API for us, saving us the effort of writing code to do the basics of connecting, authenticating, and creating REST-based calls.

As always, the first thing that we need to do is include the libraries that we require. Consider the following code snippet:

```
require 'puppet'
require 'yaml'
require 'logger'

begin
  require 'jiralicious'
rescue LoadError
  Puppet.info 'This report requires the jiralicious gem to run'
end
```

In this case, we include the usual suspects in the form of the `puppet`, `yaml`, and `logger` libraries and also include the `jiralicious` library. The `jiralicious` library deals with many of the common API calls used to interact with JIRA and saves us from having to write our own interfaces. For our simple use, this gem is a perfect fit. Now that we have our libraries, we need to register our report and load our configuration file. This is described in the following code snippet:

```
Puppet::Reports.register_report(:jiraalert) do

  def process

    @log = Logger.new('/var/log/puppet/puppetreport.log')

    configfile =
  File.join([File.dirname(Puppet.settings[:config]),
  'jiraalert.yaml'])
    raise(Puppet::ParseError, "mysqlreport configfile not
      readable") unless File.exist?(configfile)
    config = YAML.load_file(configfile)
```

For this report processor, our configuration file will look like the following:

```
username: puppetjira
password: weakpassword
uri: http://jira.fictonalco.com
apiversion: latest
authtype: basic
project: PUP
```

As you can see, the configuration of the `jiralicious` library is fairly lightweight and needs only the username, password, URI, and API version. The URI is the address of your JIRA server; this can just as easily be an on-demand instance as a locally hosted version.

Now that we have our settings, we need to connect to our JIRA instance. We call on the `jiralicious` library to do this and feed it the values it needs via our configuration file in the same way as the previous examples. Consider the following code:

```
    Jiralicious.configure do |jiraconfig|
      # Leave out username and password
  jiraconfig.username = config['username']
  jiraconfig.password = config['password']
      jiraconfig.uri = config['uri']
      jiraconfig.api_version = config['apiversion']
```

```
    jiraconfig.auth_type = config['authtype']
      end
      project = config['project']
```

Now, all we need to do is decide which events we want to send to JIRA; in this case, we're going to send any Puppet report that has a status of `failed` to JIRA as a bug. We simply pull the details we require from the Puppet report using the `.self` notation, starting with the `self.status` object. If its value is `failed`, then we construct a JSON string (Java Script Object Notation, a common data type for configuration and API calls) that contains the data we require from the transaction report. Once we've built our document, we then call the `Jiralicious::Issue.create` method and pass the document as a method argument. This is described in the following code snippet:

```
      if self.status == 'failed'
        puppet_data = {
            "fields" => {
                "project" => {
                    "key" => "#{project}"},
                "summary" => "#{self.host} Failed puppet run",
                "description" => "Host #{self.host} Failed puppet run at
  #{self.time}",
                "issuetype" => {"name" => "Bug"}}}
        Jiralicious::Issue.create(puppet_data)
      end

    rescue => err
      @log.fatal("Caught exception; exiting")
      @log.fatal(err)
    end
  end
```

Our document harvests several important pieces of data to post into JIRA. Firstly, we hand it the project that this new issue should be logged to and then add a brief summary that includes the Puppet agent host that has flagged the error. Finally, we set the issue type to be a bug.

Install this report processor in the usual way, restart your Puppet master, and keep an eye on your JIRA queue; you will find that your failed hosts are now registering themselves within JIRA, ready for the attention of a free developer. Bug tracking tools such as JIRA can be used to vastly improve your Puppet code. Tracking common issues and having a documented solution imposes a certain amount of discipline. After all, no one wants their code to be the reason that there are several hundred bug tickets waiting to be dealt with!

A final note on third-party applications

As you've seen, with the correct Ruby libraries and some creative Ruby code, you can allow Puppet to communicate with pretty much any third-party product. These days, it's almost a given that there is an API, and on the Puppet Forge, you can already see some exciting examples of report processors ranging from alerts via instant message through to logging deployment data into systems such as New Relic. When you come to look at your own report processors, be creative and remember that Puppet is rapidly becoming the first place where changes occur, which makes it the perfect early warning system for impending issues. By thinking about report processors both as a reporting mechanism and, perhaps more importantly, an alerting system, you can create some fantastic ways to keep yourself apprised of change within your Puppet-managed infrastructure.

Summary

By now, you have a good idea of what you can do with the Puppet report processor. We've taken a look at the very basics of a report processor and explored the simple steps required to create a new one. We've also investigated ways to parse the data that Puppet sends in its transaction reports and noted how the majority of the code in a report processor is generally business logic that deals with data rather than low-level connectivity code. The example code in this chapter demonstrated how there is generally a library available that can ease the development of report processors by taking care of common tasks such as connecting to databases and third-party applications.

In this chapter, we've covered how to send e-mails, export data to MySQL, and log to JIRA using existing libraries to lighten the load. We've explored different ways in which we can use the data and hopefully encouraged you to think about your own report processors.

In the next chapter, we're going to take a look at the world of PuppetDB, what it's used for, and how to go about setting it up on our Puppet servers.

5
Exploring PuppetDB

We have spent quite a bit of time looking at the basics of the Puppet reporting system and learned a fair bit about its underlying mechanisms and data formats. Now, it is time to turn our attention to PuppetDB. PuppetDB is an extremely fast data storage service that Puppet is able to utilize in preference to storing the reports elsewhere, and it offers a rich API for data discovery.

In this chapter, we're going to cover the following topics:

- A brief tour of PuppetDB and its uses
- Backend data storage options for PuppetDB
- Configuring your Puppet masters to use PuppetDB

By the end of this chapter, you should be comfortable both with what PuppetDB is used for and how to install and configure it.

A brief history of PuppetDB

Over the past few years, an awful lot of effort has gone into making Puppet perform well when scaled, and this has led to several interesting advances in the product. Not only has the catalog compilation become faster (200 times faster from version 2 to version 3), but some serious gains have been made in terms of scaling massive Puppet installations. As is often the case, this isn't just about making some things faster but also about taking a good hard look at how some components function and replacing them with something more suitable if they are found to be wanting.

Increased performance was obviously at the forefront of Puppet Labs developers' minds when they came to consider exported configurations. Exported configurations are an excellent feature in Puppet that allow a node to pass its configuration onto other nodes. This is especially handy when configuring backups, monitoring, or any other item that might need to know how another node is configured. By their very nature, exported configurations require a place to be stored; after all, a node doesn't have any idea as to which other nodes may require configuration from it, so it makes sense to store it with the Puppet master. This storage needs to be accessible, but above all, it needs to be fast. A slow exporting configuration store can seriously impact the performance of a catalog.

Originally, the Puppet master dealt with stored configuration. It would take the data from the node, store it, and when asked, it would reply to a node with the details. This worked and was simple, but was inherently slow as it introduced an expensive lookup operation to the Puppet master. It also scaled poorly, with catalogs that have large numbers of managed resources taking a lot of time to apply. Obviously, this needed improvement, and that's exactly what the Puppet Labs developers did with PuppetDB.

PuppetDB was built from the ground up to be a high-performance place to persist stored configurations in. Rather than developing it in Ruby as with the rest of Puppet, they decided to move it to an application written in Clojure. After several iterations, it was found that Clojure performed well and, as a language, had the libraries and structure to ease the development of PuppetDB.

The other technological feature worth noting with PuppetDB is its data store. By default, PuppetDB ships with an in-memory database, but this is more for the proof of concept than production use. It's a **HyperSQL Database** (**HSQLDB**) and will very quickly fill up unless you have either very few Puppet nodes or unlimited RAM (and extremely deep pockets to fund the everlasting RAM). For production use, it's highly recommended that you back PuppetDB with a PostgreSQL database; the Puppet Labs' recommendation is that this is required any time you go above a hundred nodes. Personally, I recommend it even if you have five nodes. PostgreSQL is inherently more stable, better performing, and easier to back up and maintain than HSQLDB. You can find the scaling recommendations for PuppetDB at `https://docs.puppetlabs.com/puppetdb/latest/scaling_recommendations.html`.

What if you want to use a different database?

For those of you who are fans of either MySQL or Oracle, I'm afraid you're out of luck, as PuppetDB will only run against PostgreSQL. There is the possibility of its future support with Oracle, but due to MySQL lacking support for certain key features that PuppetDB requires, the most notable being recursive queries, there is almost no chance of it being supported.

Clojure runs on top of **Java Virtual Machine (JVM)** and is a dialect of the Lisp language. Don't worry, though; you are not going to need to learn Lisp or Clojure to work with PuppetDB. This is due to a key design decision made early on in the life of PuppetDB to make the data as easily accessible as possible via the **REST API**.

PuppetDB has many of the same tunable options as most common JVM apps, so you can set the amount of the heap memory that it can consume; the official recommendation from Puppet Labs is that you allocate 128 MB of RAM if you're using PostgreSQL and at least 1 GB of heap memory if you're using an embedded database. Once it is started, PuppetDB will open a port on `8080` by default, but that's a fairly common port if you're running any other JVM-based application, so make sure that you are not going to clash before installing PuppetDB. We'll take a look at how you change the port slightly later in this chapter when we're looking at the setup of PuppetDB.

So far, all of this is interesting, but as this is a slender tome about Puppet reporting and alerting and so far PuppetDB has been all about exported configurations, this would probably not be of great interest—a footnote or an information box at best. However, there are two other things that PuppetDB stores that make it very relevant indeed to this book, and they are reports and facts.

Node facts have always been available in PuppetDB, but as of the more recent version, Version 1.4, you also have the option to use it as your reporting endpoint. This is excellent news on many levels. Firstly, it means that you are able to leverage the speed of PuppetDB when uploading reports, and secondly, it is very easy to enable it. However, what's especially interesting is that you are then able to use the PuppetDB query API to explore your data.

The PuppetDB query API is in its third version and is evolving rapidly. In its current form, it is a fantastic tool to explore any and all data about your Puppet infrastructure using an easy-to-use and very accessible RESTful API. Each version of the API has a different set of endpoints. An endpoint in PuppetDB speak is an information store; this could be, for example, the events endpoint, which is a source you can mine for details about Puppet events. Alternatively, you can look at the reports endpoint, metrics, nodes, and many more. You can fully expect each new version to expose even more data.

We're going to take a good look at the PuppetDB query API in *Chapter 6, Retrieving Data with the PuppetDB API*. For the moment, let's take a look at the steps we need to follow to get PuppetDB up and running.

Setting up the PuppetDB server

Setting up PuppetDB consists of two processes. The first process is to actually install PuppetDB and its terminus, and the second step is to get Puppet to forward data to it. None of this is especially complicated.

Installing PuppetDB

The first thing we need to do is go ahead and install PuppetDB. As always, it's best to get this from the Puppet Labs' official repos, as the Linux distribution of your choice may well be lagging behind in versions, sometimes extremely so, or may not even have PuppetDB available as a package. If you've followed the instructions from *Chapter 1, Setting Up Puppet for Reporting*, you should already be in fine form. You will also want to make sure that you have JVM installed. This can either be the **OpenJDK** shipped with your distribution, or something like the **Sun JDK**. PuppetDB will run happily with any of these.

Installing PuppetDB from packages

Once you're ready to install PuppetDB, log on to your Puppet master and issue one of the following commands:

- For Debian-based distributions, issue the following command:

  ```
  sudo apt-get install puppetdb
  ```

- For RedHat-based distributions, issue the following command:

  ```
  sudo yum install puppetdb
  ```

This will then kick off your package manager to fetch the PuppetDB application plus any prerequisites. Once it's installed, you should find that you have a new directory in the `/etc/` directory, called `puppetdb`; this is the configuration folder for PuppetDB and contains all of the configuration files that you need to get PuppetDB up and running. You will also find that you have a new service installed called PuppetDB.

Increasing the JVM heap space

At this point, you have everything you need to run PuppetDB on your server, and you could go right ahead and start it now. The trouble is, PuppetDB is in a usable but less scalable state out of the box. As mentioned earlier, PuppetDB ships with an in-memory database by default, which is heavily constrained in terms of scale by its very nature. There are two ways to approach this. Firstly, you can edit the JVM options to give the in-memory database more headroom, or secondly, you can use PostgreSQL as the backing store. Let's take a look at both techniques.

Increasing the amount of memory available to PuppetDB is a straightforward task. All of the PuppetDB JVM configurations can be found in the following directories:

- For Debian-based distributions, the configuration can be found in the following location:

  `/etc/default/puppetdb`

- For RedHat-based distributions, the configuration can be found in the following location:

  `/etc/sysconfig/puppetdb`

This file contains the fundamental settings that PuppetDB requires to work, such as the user to run it under, the aforementioned JVM options, the installation directory, and so on. You don't need to fiddle with most of these unless you've installed PuppetDB into another directory or need to run it under a different system account. The option we're interested in is `JAVA_ARGS`. The `JAVA_ARGS` option allows you to feed any JVM option to PuppetDB, but unless you have a very specific need, it's best to not tune the more esoteric settings. Improperly tuned JVM settings probably account for 50 percent of the problems that I see on Java applications.

The only setting we should work with here is the `-Xmx` setting. The `-Xmx` setting controls the maximum amount of heap memory that a Java application can use, and in the case of PuppetDB, it has to account for both the application itself plus the data if you are using the in-memory database. By default, this is set to `192m`, and depending on the size of your Puppet infrastructure, you may want to increase this using the `JAVA_ARGS="-Xmx2g"` command. The official Puppet guidelines state that once you get to around the 100 node mark, you should move to PostgreSQL. This makes sense, as HSQLDB is pretty terrible at dealing with large transactions, and at the point at which you are supporting 100 nodes, you are going to need a comparatively huge amount of RAM to support it.

Installing PostgreSQL

Setting up PostgreSQL as the PuppetDB store is a reasonably straightforward task; the packaging takes care of installing the actual database engine, leaving us to set up a new database and user. For the purposes of this example, I'm going to install PostgreSQL on my Puppet master. However, it's quite possible, if not preferable, that you run the PostgreSQL server on a separate hardware on your PuppetDB server for larger instances.

> When working with large-scale Puppet infrastructure, it's best to separate the roles, with a separate PuppetDB server, PostgreSQL server, and Puppet master. This allows you to scale each element in isolation and ensures that one component will find it hard to slow down the other.

Installing the packages

Let's go ahead and install PostgreSQL using the available packages for the following distributions:

- For Debian-based distributions, issue the following command:

  ```
  sudo apt-get install postgresql
  ```

- For RedHat-based distributions, issue the following command:

  ```
  sudo yum install postgresql
  ```

Creating your database user

Once PostgreSQL is installed, we can turn our attention to the user. To create the user, we can use the tools that have been installed along with PostgreSQL. To ensure that we do not cause problems with clashing permissions, we are going to run this as a PostgreSQL user. If we were to use another user, say the root user, we could potentially create files that the PostgreSQL user cannot access; this would cause problems, as it is the PostgreSQL user that runs the underlying service. Let's go ahead and run this as a PostgreSQL user, using the following command:

```
sudo -u postgres ssh
```

Next, let's create our user using the `createuser` command installed along with PostgreSQL, and set a secure password. This is described in the following screenshot:

```
$ createuser -DRSP puppetdb
Enter password for new role:
Enter it again:
$
```

Creating the PostgreSQL database

The final step for the initial setup is to create the database itself using the `createdb` command. This is described in the following screenshot:

```
$ createdb -E UTF8 -O puppetdb puppetdb
$
```

This command creates a new database with UTF8 encoding and ensures that our Puppet user is its owner. The UTF8 encoding is important as PuppetDB uses JSON as the format for its data, and if you don't ensure that the database is UTF8-encoded, you may find that PuppetDB runs into trouble fairly quickly. By default, the PuppetDB terminus converts strings into UTF8 encoding and expects its backend store to be able to store this data in a UTF8-encoded form.

Now that we have our database, we need to ensure that it will allow our PuppetDB to access it. PostgreSQL uses a file called `pg_hba.conf` to determine the access control to the database and the authentication method. Generally speaking, this is set to be quite secure from the installation, so we need to make some adjustments. You can find the `pg_hba.conf` file in the following places:

- For Debian-based distributions:

  `/etc/postgresql/9.1/main/pg_hba.conf`

- For RedHat-based distributions:

  `/var/lib/pgsql/data/pg_hba.conf`

Take a look inside the file with your favorite editor. The first thing that you're going to be greeted with is a wall of text; these are the comments that the PostgreSQL developers have helpfully added. These are worth a read as they set exactly how this file works. However, the block of configuration we are looking for is the following one:

```
local    all         all                          md5
host     all         all      127.0.0.1/32        md5
host     all         all      ::1/128             md5
```

If these lines do not appear in that file, then go ahead and add them, and then restart PostgreSQL. These lines essentially set access permissions that allow access to any user on any database from `127.0.0.1` (the server's local network), basically ensuring that any process running on the same server as PostgreSQL will be able to access the database. If you are running PostgreSQL on a remote server, then you will need to add a suitable access line. If in doubt, consult the handy comments at the top of the `pg_hba.conf` file.

This basically ties up all of the activity required to configure PostgreSQL, and now we just need to get PuppetDB to use it as its data store. This is done using the `/etc/puppetdb/conf.d/database.ini` configuration file. Go ahead and open it up in your editor. You will see the following configuration:

```
[database]

classname = org.hsqldb.jdbcDriver
subprotocol = hsqldb
subname =
  file:/var/lib/puppetdb/db/db;hsqldb.tx=mvcc;sql.syntax_pgs=true
username = foobar
password = foobar
gc-interval = 60
log-slow-statements = 10
```

As you can see from the preceding code file, PuppetDB is configured to use the embedded database. This is easy to change, though. The following is what the same configuration file looks like but configured for PostgreSQL:

```
[database]

classname = org.postgresql.Driver
subprotocol = postgresql
subname = localhost:5432/puppetdb
username = puppet
password = puppet
```

Amend your database configuration file to look like the preceding code and restart PuppetDB. It will now use the PostgreSQL database. Again, if you are using a remote PostgreSQL database, then you will need to amend your configuration to suit.

We have one final step and that is to install the PuppetDB terminus. The PuppetDB terminus is simply an endpoint for Puppet to connect to and must be installed on the Puppet master; this is especially important if you are running PuppetDB on a separate host. Installing the PuppetDB terminus is simple and can be done using the following commands:

- For Debian-based distributions, issue the following command:

  ```
  apt-get install puppetdb-terminus
  ```

- For RedHat-based distributions, issue the following command:

  ```
  yum install puppetdb-terminus
  ```

These commands will then fetch the `puppetdb-terminus` package and install it onto your system. Once it's installed, we need to configure our Puppet master to connect to it.

Firstly, let's create our `puppetdb.conf` file for Puppet. This is located in the same directory as your main Puppet configuration, normally, `/etc/puppet/`. If it is not already present, then go ahead and create a new file called `puppetdb.conf` in that directory. The `puppetdb.conf` file is very simple and only needs to contain a pointer to your PuppetDB instance. In my case, this will be the same server as Puppet so the file could look like the following configuration:

```
[main]
server = puppet.stunthamster.com
port = 8081
```

Next, we need to configure the Puppet master itself. This is done in the usual file, that is, the `/etc/puppet/puppet.conf` file. The configuration will sit in the `[master]` block and should look like the following configuration:

```
[master]
storeconfigs = true
storeconfigs_backend = puppetdb
```

This is enough for basic PuppetDB usage, but we also want the reports feature. This is added like any other report processor in the `reports` option and should be added as shown in the following code:

```
reports = puppetdb
```

Remember, you can have multiple report processors so PuppetDB doesn't have to be the only one, and it's indeed beneficial to have several report processors. As you will see in the next chapter, PuppetDB makes an excellent choice for reporting but lacks the ability to issue alerts. By combining the PuppetDB report processor with a suitable alerting report processor, you can have the best of both worlds.

Finally, we need to create the `routes` file. The `routes` file is required for the proper behavior of PuppetDB and allows Puppet to override certain indirection values. You probably don't have a `routes` file as yet, so go ahead and create one at `/etc/puppet/routes.yaml` and add in the following content:

```
master:
facts:
  terminus: puppetdb
  cache: yaml
```

That's it! You're all set. Simply restart your Puppet master, and it should be set to use PuppetDB.

Summary

In this chapter, we've taken a very quick look at the history and usages of PuppetDB. We've taken a look at the underlying technology that powers it and learned that although it ships with an in-memory database, the best practice when using it is to install and utilize a PostgreSQL database for its data store. We went into detail about how you can configure and install PuppetDB, from the initial package installation of PuppetDB and PostgreSQL to the details on how to configure both the products so that they can communicate.

In the next chapter, we're going to explore ways to use PuppetDB to view your data. We're going to learn how the PuppetDB API works and go through some examples of how simple and powerful it is to query this well-performing data store.

6
Retrieving Data with the PuppetDB API

In the previous chapter, we learned how to set up PuppetDB. Now, it's time to put it to work. PuppetDB is more than just a storage engine; it also contains a powerful query API that allows you to interactively query data about your Puppet infrastructure. By using a combination of REST calls with the provided query language, you will be able to find enormous amounts of data related to your Puppet-managed infrastructure.

In this chapter, we're going to take a look at the following topics:

- The hows, whats, and whys; a brief introduction to the query API
- Exploring and using endpoints
- Getting acquainted with some basic queries

By the end of this chapter, you should be fully comfortable working with the PuppetDB API and should be able to select the appropriate data sources and construct queries to explore your own data.

Exploring the PuppetDB query API

Data is only useful if you have some means to access it, and yet this is a truism that many systems seem to have forgotten, relying on developers to come along and fill whatever egregious gaps in data exploration the original product left out, instead. Fortunately, Puppet offers a rich data discovery tool in the form of the PuppetDB API and its associated query language.

As we discovered in the previous chapter, PuppetDB is more than just a place to dump data about Puppet; it's a fully functioning and high-performance endpoint that Puppet can utilize to speed up exported configuration data, catalog compilation, and more. By adding PuppetDB to your Puppet infrastructure, you will find that you will get some fantastic performance gains across almost all parts of the product as well as gaining a powerful reporting endpoint.

One of the key decisions made by the PuppetDB developers was to make the data that PuppetDB holds accessible by a well-documented and powerful API. This makes it possible to create your own applications to leverage the data that your Puppet-managed infrastructure has sent Puppet without needing to design your own storage and query mechanism. Although it's powerful, the PuppetDB API has a complex query language that can take some time to get accustomed to.

The PuppetDB query API and especially the query language can be a complex topic, but the developers have provided some excellent documentation. You can find the documentation at `https://docs.puppetlabs.com/puppetdb/latest/`.

The PuppetDB API is, in fact, split into two distinct functions: the query interface and the command interface. The majority of this chapter will deal with the query interface, but it's worth exploring what the command interface is and what it is used for.

Understanding the command interface

The command interface is normally not used directly, so we're not going to go into any great detail on how it is used. There is almost no circumstance under which you would directly use the command interface as the only vaguely useful command would be the `deactivate node` command, and even then, this is best left for PuppetDB and Puppet to deal with.

The command interface offers the following functions:

- `replace catalog`: This command is used when a fresh set of data is received from the Puppet client, and it replaces the previously held data for this node
- `replace facts`: This function takes incoming facts from a node and replaces the stored facts with the latest version
- `store report`: This is a new feature with v3 of the API and allows PuppetDB to act as a report processor for storing reports and events
- `deactivate node`: This will mark a node as inactive within PuppetDB and make it eligible for housekeeping next time the database is compacted

> Node deactivation is an important part of PuppetDB's housekeeping. While nodes are active, their configuration will be exported along with all other exported resources. When you are dealing with catalogs of thousands of nodes, it's important that the old ones be marked as deactivated so that their data isn't considered. This is especially important if you are using a dynamic environment that treats nodes as ephemeral and creates and destroys them at will. Periodically, PuppetDB will run a garbage-collection sweep; this is essentially a housekeeping task that will remove unwanted data to keep the database small and agile.

The command interface is an HTTP call to Puppet DB and contains data in the correct PuppetDB wire format. This will change depending on what you are interacting with (resource, node, and so on) but will essentially comprise of the command plus the data wrapped in a JSON-formatted package.

> There really is no reason to use the command interface directly; however, it's important to know that it is there and how it works. It's possible in later versions of PuppetDB that new features may be introduced that add more reasons to work with the command interface, so it's good to understand the basics.

Understanding the query API interface

Now that we understand how the PuppetDB API is used to insert data, it's time to move on to a more useful topic, that is, how to retrieve data.

The PuppetDB query API is now into its third revision and has introduced some powerful new features around the reporting elements of PuppetDB. A major new feature is the ability to use PuppetDB as a report processor within the Puppet master; this is an important addition to PuppetDB as previously it could only be used to store configurations. Now, it is able to form the central hub of a powerful reporting tool, and unlike other reporting methods, PuppetDB has the advantage of both having a data store that is tuned for the task in hand and a query language that is designed for the specific role of retrieving the Puppet data.

The query API organizes its data around the concept of an endpoint. Each endpoint is essentially a data source that offers a set of RESTful routes that allow you to interact with the data. As of v3, the following endpoints are available:

- `facts`
- `resources`

- `nodes`
- `fact-names`
- `metrics`
- `reports`
- `events`
- `event-counts`
- `aggregate-event-counts`
- `version`
- `catalogs`
- `server-time`

Each endpoint is tuned to a specific task, and it's important that you select the correct one when issuing your queries. There is some potential overlap in some of the data that the endpoints offer. For example, some of the data inside the `facts` endpoint can also be found in the `nodes` endpoint. The difference lies in how the data is presented and described; for instance, if you are interested in a specific fact, including which nodes have that fact present, then you would use the `facts` endpoint. Alternatively, if you want to find out the value of a specific fact on a certain node, then you would use the `nodes` endpoint.

Once you have selected an endpoint, you can make a call to one of its available routes. A route is an HTTP path that will return a certain type of information depending on the endpoint you are interrogating. These calls should take the following form:

```
http://<server>:<puppetdbport>/<api_version>/<route>
```

When we come to look at the endpoints in detail, you will find that I've listed the available routes and the URL for the documentation. It's worth reading through the documentation for a complete list of available data from each endpoint.

Be careful with the API version. Each revision has brought a new functionality; for instance, v2 lacked most of the reporting functionality that v3 integrates. If you target the wrong version, you may either fetch unexpected data or no data at all.

When you make an API call, PuppetDB will fetch the requested data and return it in the form of a JSON response. The actual structure of the JSON document will vary depending on the endpoint used, and it's wise to consult the endpoint documentation to find out the exact format to be expected.

We are going to take a more detailed look at the available endpoints further along in this chapter, but first, we are going to spend some time looking at the PuppetDB query language.

A primer on the PuppetDB query language

With most of the endpoints, you can use the supplied routes to retrieve information. For example, the following query will return all nodes that run Linux:

```
curl http://puppetdbhost:8080/v3/facts/kernel/Linux
```

A great deal of data can be fetched using this technique, but it lacks the flexibility to reflect more complex requirements. To allow users to specify more complex queries, PuppetDB allows for some endpoints to make use of a query language within the PuppetDB API. A PuppetDB query that uses the query language is similar to a call to a route in that it is made up of an HTTP request but differs in that you supply an additional query string that contains the PuppetDB query.

PuppetDB queries can be quite complex at first glance, as they are written in reverse polish notation and are contained within a JSON array. This is somewhat different to most languages you may be used to and can take some practice to become accustomed to. Essentially, this means that each query you construct starts with the operator with any subsequent element being made up of arguments. These are then evaluated in the order they are written in. Let's see how this works in practice; take a look at the following query:

```
curl -X GET http://puppetdbhost:8080/v3/facts/processorcount --
  data-urlencode 'query=["<", "value", 2]'
```

In this example, we start with a query to the `facts` endpoint and use the route to bring back all the `processorcount` facts. We then apply a query to narrow down the result set to only nodes that have less than two processors by applying the < operator to the value field of the results from the returned data.

Let's take a look at another, more complex query. In this example, we are going to issue a query to the `resources` endpoint and use a set of queries to narrow down our data:

```
curl -X GET http://puppetdbhost:8080/v3/resources --data-urlencode
  'query=["and",["=", "type", "User"],["not",["and",["=", "type",
  "User"], ["=", "title", "mvd"]]]]'
```

In this example, we are using the `resources` endpoint to query all managed resources; we're then limiting the result set by applying a series of queries. We're using an `and` operator to join two JSON arrays, with each array containing a sub query. This query can also be represented by this: *select all resources where type equals user and exclude those where type equals user and title equals mvd*. Or, to put it another way, it can be represented by this: *find me all users, but not if they have a title of mvd*.

As you can see, the notation of the PuppetDB queries can become quite complex, but it offers a great deal of power. The best approach when constructing new queries is to build them one section at a time, check the output, and then add another. You can find more details about the available operators for queries at `http://docs.puppetlabs.com/puppetdb/latest/api/query/v3/operators.html`. It's well worth both studying the documentation and practicing queries until you are comfortable using the PuppetDB query language.

Exploring endpoints

The endpoints are the core of the PuppetDB query API, and in the next section, we are going to look at the endpoints that are available in a little more detail, which are the routes that they have made available, and how you might use them. Again, taking time to acquaint yourself with each endpoint by running some test queries is a valuable exercise, especially when examining the format of the returned data.

Using the facts endpoint

The `facts` endpoint allows you to find the fact data reported by Puppet-managed nodes to PuppetDB, including any custom facts that you have defined. The `facts` endpoint supports the following routes:

- `GET /v3/facts`
- `GET /v3/facts/<NAME>`
- `GET /v3/facts/<NAME>/<VALUE>`

As you can see, these routes offer you a simple mechanism to query your facts. For example, the following query would retrieve all IP addresses that have been assigned to any Puppet-managed node:

```
curl http://puppetdbhost:8080/v3/facts/ipaddress
```

You can insert any fact name into the path and use it to retrieve data that may be of interest. You can also add a further value after the desired fact to narrow it down to specific data, and this can allow you to zero in on interesting aspects of your infrastructure. For example, we can retrieve all hosts that run Linux by using the following query:

```
curl http://puppetdbhost:8080/v3/facts/kernel/Linux
```

> Try the preceding query again, but instead of `Linux`, use `linux`. You'll notice that this time round, you've not had any data returned; this is because facts are case sensitive within PuppetDB queries, so it's very important that you ensure you use the correct case when issuing queries.

Using the routes available in the `facts` endpoint can give you access to a wide range of data, and the available routes can be further supplemented with the addition of a PuppetDB query. For example, if we want to find all facts for a certain node, we can do so using the following query:

```
curl -X GET http://puppetdbhost:8080/v3/facts --data-urlencode
  'query=["=", "certname", "puppetagent.localdomain"]'
```

This query will produce the output shown in the following screenshot:


```
[ {
  "certname" : "puppetagent.localdomain",
  "name" : "_timestamp",
  "value" : "2014-03-02 17:38:39 +0000"
}, {
  "certname" : "puppetagent.localdomain",
  "name" : "architecture",
  "value" : "amd64"
}, {
  "certname" : "puppetagent.localdomain",
  "name" : "augeasversion",
  "value" : "1.1.0"
}, {
  "certname" : "puppetagent.localdomain",
  "name" : "bios_release_date",
  "value" : "07/31/2013"
}, {
  "certname" : "puppetagent.localdomain",
  "name" : "bios_vendor",
  "value" : "Phoenix Technologies LTD"
}, {
```

You can find the documentation for the `facts` endpoint at `https://docs.puppetlabs.com/puppetdb/latest/api/query/v3/facts.html`.

Using the resources endpoint

The `resources` endpoint allows you to query all resources that Puppet is currently managing on active nodes. PuppetDB will not respond with data for deactivated nodes. The `resources` endpoint offers the following routes:

- `GET /V3/resources/v3/resources`
- `GET /v3/resources/<TYPE>`
- `GET /v3/resources/<TYPE>/<TITLE>`

The `resources` endpoint is similar to the `facts` endpoint in its usage. The first route will return every single resource that Puppet has ever encountered, but this is of limited use and by adding a type, we can start drilling in specific details. For instance, by using the following query, you can retrieve a list of all files that Puppet is currently managing on active nodes:

```
curl http://puppetdbhost:8080/v3/resources/File
```

This example gives you the output shown in the following screenshot:

```
  "certname" : "tomcat.localdomain",
  "resource" : "fea74503471d385c9bf7470900d16adb66a392a4",
  "title" : "/etc/sudoers.d/",
  "parameters" : {
    "backup" : false,
    "mode" : "0550",
    "path" : "/etc/sudoers.d",
    "require" : "Package[sudo]",
    "purge" : true,
    "alias" : [ "/etc/sudoers.d" ],
    "ignore" : [ ".ignore", ".svn", ".git", "CVS", ".git_dont_delete", ".git_placeholder" ],
    "owner" : "root",
    "replace" : true,
    "ensure" : "directory",
    "recurse" : true,
    "group" : "root"
  },
  "type" : "File",
  "exported" : false,
  "line" : 111,
  "file" : "/etc/puppet/modules/sudo/manifests/init.pp",
  "tags" : [ "conf", "sudo::conf" ]
}, {
  "certname" : "musical.localdomain",
  "resource" : "0e85f26734d8510fffcd8c31a40e148ccc2b1484",
  "title" : "/etc/default/sensu",
  "parameters" : {
    "backup" : false,
    "mode" : "0444",
```

As with the `facts` endpoint, case matters here as well. All resources should be capitalized, so you will find that `File` will work, but `file` will return no results.

As you can see from the output shown in the preceding screenshot, the `resources` endpoint will return the name of the Puppet manifest where the resources are declared and the line on which the declaration is made. This makes it an absolute cinch to find out where resources are being defined without having to search through the code itself.

The `resources` endpoint also supports the PuppetDB query language, and you can use this to drill down to interesting data. For instance, if you want to find all files except `/etc/hosts`, you can use the following query:

```
curl -X GET http://puppetdbhost:8080/v3/resources/File --data-
  urlencode 'query=["and", ["not",["=", "title",
  "/etc/hosts"]],["=", "type", "File"]]'
```

You can find the documentation for the `resources` endpoint at `https://docs.puppetlabs.com/puppetdb/latest/api/query/v3/resources.html`.

Retrieving details about nodes

The `nodes` endpoint completes the trinity of resources, facts, and nodes, and gives you the ability to find specific information regarding nodes from PuppetDB quickly and easily. There are many aspects that you can query nodes for, and to reflect this, the `nodes` endpoint has a comparatively large set of routes compared to other endpoints. The following routes are offered by the `nodes` endpoint:

- `GET /v3/nodes`
- `GET /v3/nodes/<NODE>`
- `GET /v3/nodes/<NODE>/facts/<NAME>`
- `GET /v3/nodes/<NODE>/facts/<NAME>/<VALUE>`
- `GET /v3/nodes/<NODE>/resources`
- `GET /v3/nodes/<NODE>/resources/<TYPE>`
- `GET /v3/nodes/<NODE>/resources/<TYPE>/<TITLE>`

As you can see from the routes, you are able to retrieve both facts and resources from the `nodes` endpoint, and the response format will vary depending on which of the two you are retrieving. The ability to respond with both facts and resources makes the `nodes` endpoint incredibly versatile, and as a result, you will probably find that you use this endpoint more than the others.

Using the provided routes makes retrieving node information a straightforward task. For example, to see the basic information that PuppetDB holds about a particular node, we can call the nodes' route and supply the fully qualified domain name of the node that we are interested in. This is described in the following query:

```
curl http://puppetdbhost:8080/v3/nodes/puppetagent
```

This query gives you the output shown in the following screenshot:

```
{
  "name" : "puppetagent.localdomain",
  "deactivated" : null,
  "catalog_timestamp" : "2014-03-02T17:38:40.094Z",
  "facts_timestamp" : "2014-03-02T17:38:39.510Z",
  "report_timestamp" : null
```

Likewise, using the `nodes` endpoint and querying for facts, we can also view the versions of Facter available on a given node. This is described in the following query:

```
curl http://puppetdbhost:8080/v3/nodes/puppetagent.localdomain/
  facts/facterversion
```

This query gives you the output shown in the following screenshot:

```
[ {
  "certname" : "puppetagent.localdomain",
  "name" : "facterversion",
  "value" : "1.7.3"
} ]
```

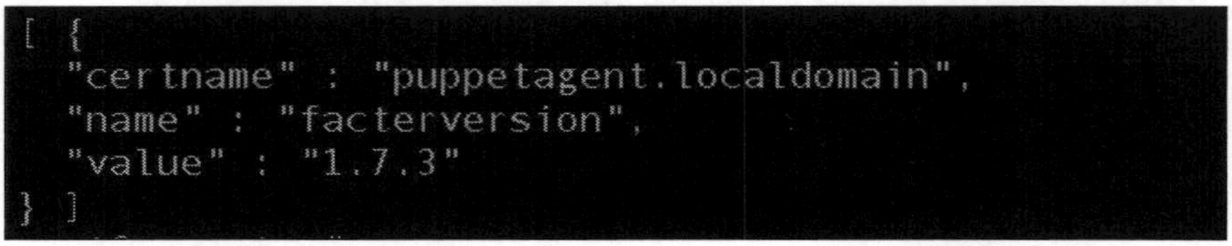

As you can see, the `nodes` endpoint allows you to drill down into the details about a specific node, but this is not limited to facts; we can retrieve details of resources as well. This can be done using the following query:

```
curl http://puppetdbhost:8080/v3/nodes/puppetagent.localdomain
  /resources/File
```

This code gives us the output shown in the following screenshot:

```
[ {
  "certname" : "puppetagent.localdomain",
  "resource" : "f7f2a2f7c1739eada7559976950da1face9f1396",
  "title" : "/etc/passwd",
  "parameters" : {
    "audit" : [ "group", "mode", "owner" ]
  },
  "type" : "File",
  "exported" : false,
  "line" : 18,
  "file" : "/etc/puppet/modules/git/manifests/init.pp",
  "tags" : [ "default", "node", "git", "class", "file" ]
} ]
```

Using the provided routes within the `nodes` endpoint gives you a fantastically powerful way to interrogate your infrastructure, but it can occasionally be limiting. Using the routes, you're not able to find a range of data. For instance, you may want to find all nodes that have more than 2 GB of RAM. Although you cannot do it using one of the standard routes, the `nodes` endpoint also supports the PuppetDB query language. Consider the following query:

```
curl -X GET http://puppetdbhost:8080/v3/nodes --data-urlencode
  'query=[">",["fact", "memorysize_mb"], "2048"]']
```

This query gives you the output shown in the following screenshot:

```
[ {
  "name" : "numbercruncher.localdomain",
  "deactivated" : null,
  "catalog_timestamp" : "2014-04-16T08:25:57.610Z",
  "facts_timestamp" : "2014-04-16T08:25:55.530Z",
  "report_timestamp" : null
}, {
  "name" : "bigmem.localdomain",
  "deactivated" : null,
  "catalog_timestamp" : "2014-04-16T13:18:32.023Z",
  "facts_timestamp" : "2014-04-16T13:18:30.162Z",
  "report_timestamp" : null
} ]
```

Getting the run details with the catalogs endpoint

The `catalogs` endpoint will retrieve the details of the last catalog to be applied to a node and currently has the following available route:

- GET /v3/catalogs/<NODE>

An example of a `catalogs` endpoint query would look like the following:

```
curl http://puppetdb:8080/v3/catalogs/puppetagent.localdomain
```

The output of this query is shown in the following screenshot:

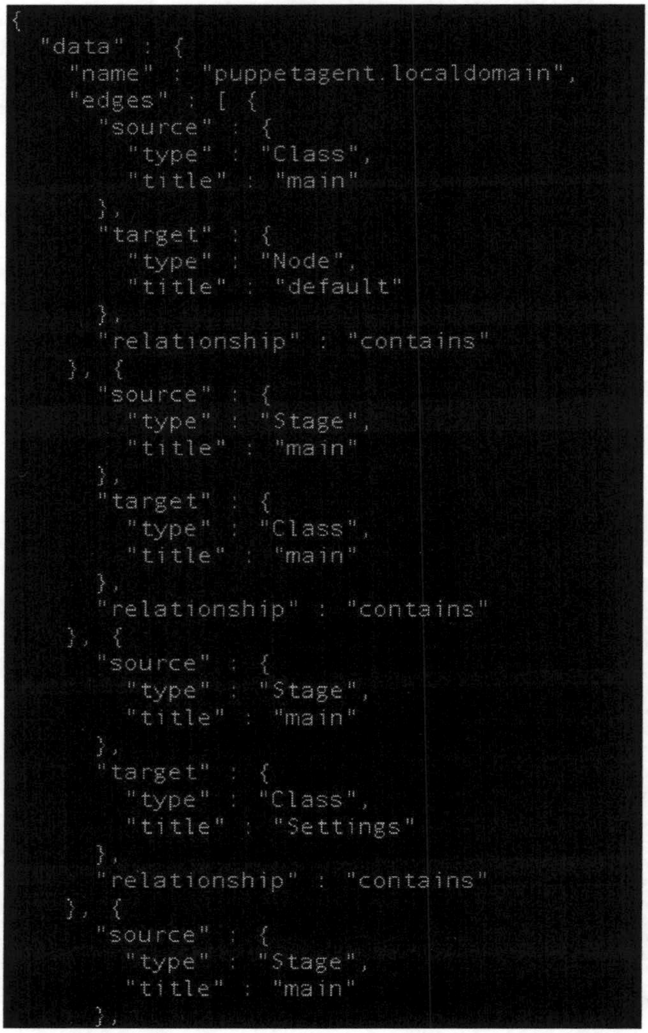

```
{
  "data" : {
    "name" : "puppetagent.localdomain",
    "edges" : [ {
      "source" : {
        "type" : "Class",
        "title" : "main"
      },
      "target" : {
        "type" : "Node",
        "title" : "default"
      },
      "relationship" : "contains"
    }, {
      "source" : {
        "type" : "Stage",
        "title" : "main"
      },
      "target" : {
        "type" : "Class",
        "title" : "main"
      },
      "relationship" : "contains"
    }, {
      "source" : {
        "type" : "Stage",
        "title" : "main"
      },
      "target" : {
        "type" : "Class",
        "title" : "Settings"
      },
      "relationship" : "contains"
    }, {
      "source" : {
        "type" : "Stage",
        "title" : "main"
      },
```

The `catalogs` endpoint allows you to retrieve the details of the Puppet catalog for a given node from its last Puppet agent run. The `catalogs` endpoint returns the data in the catalog wire format and contains both the Puppet-managed resources and their relation to each other.

> The catalog wire format can be a little complex at first glance; however, it is well documented. You can find the documentation for the catalog wire format at `http://docs.puppetlabs.com/puppetdb/latest/api/wire_format/catalog_format_v4.html`.

Querying the `catalogs` endpoint gives you an immediate sense of what has been configured on a node and allows you to easily see whether certain resources have been applied or are available. Currently, the `catalogs` endpoint does not support the query syntax; however, you can easily combine the query with the Unix `grep` command to find the data that you're interested in.

The `catalogs` endpoint returns its data in the form of a JSON map and offers two keys: the metadata key and the data key. At the moment, the metadata key contains a single piece of information, which is the version of the API. The data key contains the interesting data, and it is also made up of a JSON map that contains the catalog data in the wire format.

The `catalogs` endpoint is an excellent way to explore the state of a given node at any point of time, and it could potentially form part of a powerful auditing tool if the information is persisted to another data store and then used to compare configuration changes over time. For instance, using this technique, you could easily view when a particular application was added to a node or when a configuration file was changed.

Understanding the fact-names endpoint

You can query the `fact-names` endpoint to find the name of any facts that Puppet clients have reported in the course of their run; this includes deactivated nodes. Note that this doesn't include the actual value of the facts but just the name of the facts themselves. This can be very helpful if you want to find out whether certain custom facts have been saved into PuppetDB, or simply to explore the facts that are available to be queried. The `fact-names` endpoint currently only supports one route, which is the following one:

- `GET /fact-names`

The `fact-names` endpoint does not support any additional routes or support queries, and it will return all fact names in alphabetical order, both for active and inactive nodes. Consider the following query:

```
curl -X GET http://puppetdbhost:8080/v3/fact-names
```

This query gives you the output shown in the following screenshot:

Knowing the status of PuppetDB with the metrics endpoint

The `metrics` endpoint is your window to the performance and status of PuppetDB itself and should not be confused with the Puppet metrics, which are found in the `events` endpoint. The `metrics` endpoint is interesting as it exposes its data in the form of Java-managed beans (MBeans). These are part of the Java management extensions and are commonly used by various applications to gather statistical information. These are especially prevalent in the monitoring world. You're not limited to using MBeans, though, as a standard API call will also return the information—be warned, though; this may be a huge amount of information and you may end up running into issues that require you to make use of the paging option.

> The paging option allows you to sort the returned information and, more importantly, limit the amount of results. Most PuppetDB queries support paging and when faced with a huge amount of results, it can be very useful. You can find the details for paging at `http://docs.puppetlabs.com/puppetdb/latest/api/query/v3/paging.html`.

The `metrics` endpoint can be useful to gauge how well your PuppetDB is performing, how many resources it's currently managing, and how quickly it is servicing requests. For example, you can query the `metrics` endpoint to find out the number of nodes that are currently reporting to PuppetDB. This is described in the following query:

```
curl -G 'http://localhost:8080/v3/metrics/mbean/com.puppetlabs
  .puppetdb.query.population:type=default,name=num-nodes'
```

We can also examine how quickly PuppetDB is replying to our queries, and this can serve as an early warning that you need to increase the resources available to the server if it has started to run a little sluggishly.

There is a wealth of information available in the `metrics` endpoint, and it is an excellent point to add monitoring. By monitoring the metrics, you are able to respond proactively to any slowdowns in your Puppet infrastructure and scale accordingly.

You can find the documentation for the `metrics` endpoint at `http://docs.puppetlabs.com/puppetdb/latest/api/query/v3/metrics.html`.

Using the reports endpoint

The `reports` endpoint offers a summary version of the Puppet report for each of the active nodes within your Puppet-managed infrastructure. Note that this is a summary of the report rather than the full report itself, and currently, it only has the following single route:

- `/v3/reports`

The `reports` endpoint is very useful for seeing when a node last performed a Puppet transaction, and, of course, it gives you the all important hash that allows you to tie this report to the underlying events.

The report hash is something you will find yourself using often, as it is your link from the Puppet report to the individual events that make up the transaction. Using the hash provided by the `reports` endpoint, you can query the `events` endpoint to gather the events that occurred during a Puppet run.

Although it only has a single route, it requires the use of the PuppetDB query language, albeit limited to an equality (=) operator; if you do not supply a query, then it will return no data. A basic query looks like the following one:

```
curl -G 'http://localhost:8080/v3/reports' --data-urlencode
  'query=["=", "certname", "puppet.localdomain"]'
```

This code gives you the output shown in the following screenshot:


```
[ {
  "end-time" : "2014-05-06T23:49:32.256Z",
  "certname" : "puppetagent.localdomain",
  "hash" : "60063c269ed6b066c331f838e9588fee0a0b9f7c",
  "report-format" : 4,
  "start-time" : "2014-05-06T23:49:20.511Z",
  "puppet-version" : "3.5.1",
  "configuration-version" : "1399379848",
  "transaction-uuid" : "4e06d011-9f23-4083-97d2-5af9bc16ec24",
  "receive-time" : "2014-05-06T23:49:50.980Z"
}, {
  "end-time" : "2014-05-06T23:19:31.671Z",
  "certname" : "puppetagent.localdomain",
  "hash" : "5cfe6f165950a20ebb8b7f57207359fc2d353916",
  "report-format" : 4,
  "start-time" : "2014-05-06T23:19:20.499Z",
  "puppet-version" : "3.5.1",
  "configuration-version" : "1399379848",
  "transaction-uuid" : "d212c4d5-f47a-4732-add0-f052302cb6c5",
  "receive-time" : "2014-05-06T23:19:50.720Z"
} ]
```


The `reports` endpoint should be your starting point when you come to examine events that affect your nodes. From here, you can then delve into the `events` endpoint to gather any details you need. You can find the documentation for the `reports` endpoint at `http://docs.puppetlabs.com/puppetdb/latest/api/query/v3/reports.html`.

Working with the events endpoint

Much like the traditional reporting mechanism, the `events` endpoint gives us access to events from a Puppet client run. Currently, the `events` endpoint only supports a single route, which is the following one:

- `GET /v3/events`

The `events` endpoint is similar to the `reports` endpoint in that it requires the use of a query to return any data. However, unlike the `reports` endpoint, it supports the full range of operators within the query. This means that you can use the `events` endpoint to find out details such as events during a certain time period or events that failed to be applied. It also allows you to take the hash from the `reports` endpoint and see all the events that took place, as shown in the following example query:

```
curl -G 'http://puppetdbhost:8080/v3/events' --data-urlencode
  'query=["=", "report",
  "7eb94f7b8e89e1597672f190d864243543b3ac48"]'
```

This query gives you the output shown in the following screenshot:

```
[ {
  "status" : "failure",
  "timestamp" : "2014-04-29T08:19:02.894Z",
  "certname" : "puppetagent.localdomain",
  "containing-class" : "musicapp",
  "containment-path" : [ "Stage[main]", "musicapp", "Exec[app-stable]" ],
  "report" : "a699c81ede0644e25f6f3a33b121636396da2a30",
  "run-start-time" : "2014-04-29T08:18:44.613Z",
  "resource-title" : "app-stable",
  "configuration-version" : "1398697611",
  "run-end-time" : "2014-04-29T08:18:52.148Z",
  "property" : "returns",
  "message" : "Unable to start app - groove failure",
  "new-value" : [ "0" ],
  "old-value" : "notrun",
  "line" : 26,
  "file" : "/etc/puppet/modules/musicapp/manifests/init.pp",
  "report-receive-time" : "2014-04-29T08:19:12.510Z",
  "resource-type" : "Exec"
}, {
  "status" : "skipped",
  "timestamp" : "2014-04-29T08:19:03.714Z",
  "certname" : "puppetagent.localdomain",
  "containing-class" : "disco",
  "containment-path" : [ "Stage[main]", "disco", "Package[disco-app]" ],
```


The `events` endpoint is a versatile way of finding out which declared resources are having difficulties. For example, we can find resources that have failed to get themselves applied by using the following query:

```
curl -G 'http://puppetdbhost:8080/v3/events' --data-urlencode
  'query=["=", "status", "failure"]'
```

You will find yourself using the `events` endpoint quite often, and once you are comfortable with some of the more common queries such as the preceding query, you will find that it is a quick way to find extremely valuable information about your Puppet-managed infrastructure. The documentation has many more examples and can be found at `http://docs.puppetlabs.com/puppetdb/latest/api/query/v3/events.html`.

Using the event-counts endpoint

When you issue a query to the `event-counts` endpoint, you provide it with the resource, class, or node that you're interested in. PuppetDB will then return you a list of how many times that resource has been in the success, failure, noop, or skip status.

Currently, the `event-counts` endpoint supports a single route, which is the following one:

- `/v3/event-counts`

The `event-counts` endpoint is built on top of the `events` endpoint, and therefore, all the query operators you can use with the `events` endpoint are applicable here. The following example queries the host `puppetagent.localdomain` for any resource that has any failures, and then summarizes how many failures occurred by that resource:

```
curl -G 'http://puppetdbhost:8080/v3/event-counts'--data-
  urlencode'query=["=", "certname", "puppetagent.localdomain"]' --
  data-urlencode 'counts-filter=[">", "failures", 0]' --data-
  urlencode 'summarize-by=resource'
```

This query gives you the output shown in the following screenshot:

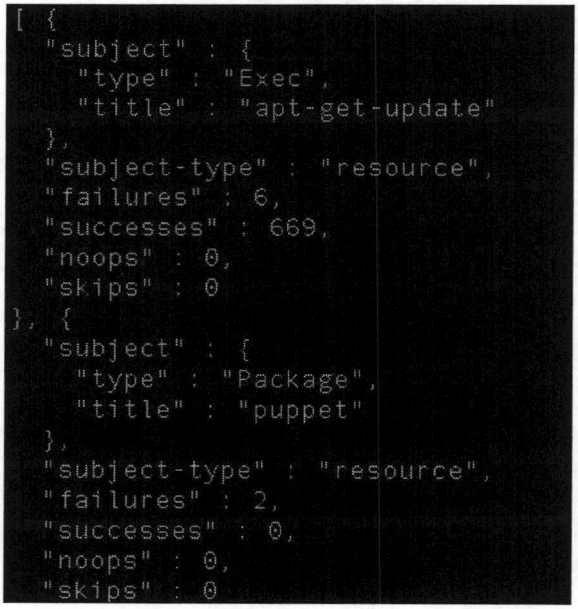

```
[ {
  "subject" : {
    "type" : "Exec",
    "title" : "apt-get-update"
  },
  "subject-type" : "resource",
  "failures" : 6,
  "successes" : 669,
  "noops" : 0,
  "skips" : 0
}, {
  "subject" : {
    "type" : "Package",
    "title" : "puppet"
  },
  "subject-type" : "resource",
  "failures" : 2,
  "successes" : 0,
  "noops" : 0,
  "skips" : 0
```

You can find the documentation and more examples for the `event-counts` endpoint at `http://docs.puppetlabs.com/puppetdb/latest/api/query/v3/event-counts.html`.

Applying the aggregate-event-counts endpoint

This is an aggregated version of the `event-counts` endpoint; it supports the same fields as the `event-counts` endpoint as it is essentially an extension of that endpoint. This can be very handy if you are developing some custom reporting, as it saves you having to aggregate the data yourself; nine times out of ten, it's faster and easier to leave this to PuppetDB. Currently, the `aggregate-event-counts` endpoint supports a single route, which is the following one:

- `GET /v3/aggregate-event-counts`

You can find the documentation for the `aggregate-event-counts` endpoint at `http://docs.puppetlabs.com/puppetdb/2.0/api/query/v3/aggregate-event-counts.html`.

Using the server-time endpoint

This endpoint may well make you wonder what it's for; however, it's a very useful endpoint when you're trying to figure out what happened during a very specific time period. At present, it supports a single route, which is the following one:

- `GET /v3/server-time`

The trouble with times on servers is that they can drift, and even with **Network Time Protocol (NTP)**, they can produce markedly different responses. The `server-time` endpoint allows you to find the current time from the point of view of the Puppet master; this can be quite important if you are querying for time-based information, as it gives you an accurate starting point rather than a possibly skewed value based on the current time on your desktop. You can retrieve the server time with the following simple query:

```
curl http://puppetdbhost:8080/v3/server-time
```

You can also find the documentation for this endpoint at `http://docs.puppetlabs.com/puppetdb/latest/api/query/v3/server-time.html`.

The version endpoint

This is a straightforward endpoint and is useful if you want to know the version of PuppetDB that you are running. This can be extremely useful if you want to ensure that your application is using the correct version of the API. You can essentially check whether the PuppetDB server is running the version you expect, and if not, you can either bail out or handle the difference another way. Currently, the `version` endpoint supports a single route, which is the following one:

- `GET /v3/version`

To find the version of your Puppet master, you can use the following query:

```
curl http://localhost:8080/v3/version
```

You can find the documentation for the `version` endpoint at `http://docs.puppetlabs.com/puppetdb/latest/api/query/v3/version.html`.

Summary

In this chapter, we have fully explored the PuppetDB API. We've taken a look at the role that the API endpoints play and how you can use simple command-line tools to query it. We've examined the makeup of a typical query and how we can use operators to be selective about our data. Finally, we've taken a look at some of the more practical ways in which we can put the PuppetDB query API to use, and we have examined how it can be used to increase the visibility of your infrastructure.

In the next chapter, we're going to use some simple Ruby code to create a simple reporting system, utilizing the features of the PuppetDB API to power it.

7
Writing Custom Reports with PuppetDB

In the previous chapter, we learned about the PuppetDB query API, what it can be used for, and how to leverage the power of its built-in query language. In this chapter, we're going to take that knowledge and use it to create a simple but effective reporting application written in Ruby. We're going to explore the following topics:

- Creating a skeleton Ruby application
- Connecting to PuppetDB using JSON
- Retrieving facts
- Retrieving events and reports using multiple endpoints

At the end of this chapter, you should be comfortable making use of the PuppetDB query API in your own applications and understand how to process the JSON output of the API.

Creating a basic query application

We're going to start with a simple application to explore the PuppetDB API. This will get us acquainted with the basic tools that we need to access the API and extract data from it. Open your favorite editor and create a new file called `basic_report.rb`.

The basic report application is going to be very straightforward and will simply pull back some basic details about a host using the `facts` endpoint. This will demonstrate the basic techniques we're going to use to write a more fully featured application later on in this chapter.

> The code in this chapter has been designed to run against Ruby v1.9 and above, and it will throw errors if it's run on earlier versions. If you're using a RedHat-based distribution prior to RedHat Enterprise Linux 7, then you will almost certainly be running a version of Ruby 1.8. If you are running one of these operating systems, then I recommend that you use Ruby Version Manager (`https://rvm.io`) to install a more recent version of Ruby to run this code against.

Setting up the basic application

The first thing that we will need to do is include some additional libraries to allow us to easily parse the data that the PuppetDB API returns. As you will recall from the previous chapter, the PuppetDB API is a simple JSON feed presented over HTTP; luckily, Ruby already includes both a library to parse JSON (`json`) and a library to connect to an HTTP server (`net::HTTP`). Finally, we're going to need a library that will allow us to insert a custom parameter into our HTTP call; this is to allow us to append a PuppetDB query and is supplied by the URI library (`uri`).

Let's go ahead and start off our code by adding these libraries:

```
require 'rubygems'
require 'json'
require 'net/http'
require 'uri'
```

That's great! We've got all the tools we need to work with PuppetDB right there. The next thing we need to do is connect to the API and retrieve the response. First of all, though, we need the user of the application to let us know the node that they're interested in. We'll grab their response using the `gets` method and then use the `chomp` string function to remove any character returns from the response, as shown in the following code snippet:

```
puts 'Please input the FQDN of the node to examine:'
fqdn = gets.chomp
```

Connecting to PuppetDB

We now have the tools to access our PuppetDB data and the details of what our user wants to see. Let's connect to PuppetDB and fetch the data. The first thing we need to do is construct our **Universal Resource Identifier** (**URI**). We're going to keep things simple and hardcode the address of our Puppet master for the moment, as shown in the following code snippet:

```
uri = URI.parse('http://puppetdbhost:8080/v3/facts/')
```

This creates a variable to hold our URI; note that the URI contains not only the address of the Puppet master, but also the protocol, port, and path to the particular endpoint we're interested in.

Now, we need to construct a query to ensure that the data we return is only for the host that the user is interested in, rather than the default value of all hosts. We do this by appending a query string to the HTTP request, and this is achieved using the URI's query function. This essentially allows you to build a simple hash that contains the name of the query string and the query itself. Let's go ahead and use this to construct a query that returns just the node that our user has specified. Consider the following code:

```
params = {:query => '["=","certname",'+'"'"#{fqdn}" + '"' ']'}
uri.query = URI.encode_www_form(params)
```

The preceding query is fairly straightforward. The first line creates a variable called `params`, which contains our basic query syntax (in this case, an equality operator on the `certname` data) and the value of the `fqdn` variable that the user created by answering our prompt.

We now have all the data we need to create a connection to PuppetDB and query the database. All we have to do now is construct the HTTP call itself. Let's go ahead and do that now. This is shown in the following code snippet:

```
response = Net::HTTP.get_response(uri)
json = JSON.parse(response.body)
```

This code calls PuppetDB using the `Net::HTTP` library and then parses the resulting JSON response into a Ruby hash ready for us to work with.

Outputting results

Finally, we just need to output the results. We could simply output the results as a list, but as we're designing this application for nontechnical users, let's go ahead and make it a bit prettier. There are several Ruby gems that can be used to take the output and make it a little easier on the eye. In this case, I'm going to use a gem called `command_line_reporter`. You can install this gem in the usual manner using the following command:

```
gem install command_line_reporter
```

The next thing we need to do is include it in our application. Edit your list of included libraries as shown in the following code:

```
require 'rubygems'
require 'json'
require 'net/http'
require 'uri'
require 'command_line_reporter'
include CommandLineReporter
```

Once you've done this, you're all ready to create a good-looking report. Let's go ahead and retrieve our details and then output them using the following code:

```
table(:border => true) do
  json.each do |fact|
    row do
      column(fact['name'], :width => 20)
      column(fact['value'], :width => 60,
             :align => 'right',
             :padding => 5)
    end
  end
end
```

In this code, the first thing that we do is use the `table` method in the `command_line_reporter` library to create a table with a border; next, we create a Ruby block using the contents of the JSON response as the array. As we iterate through the array, we create a new table row for each piece of data in the array and populate it with the name and value of the facts returned by PuppetDB.

That's all we need for this program. You should have something that looks a little like the following code:

```
require "rubygems"
require "json"
require 'net/http'
require 'uri'
require 'command_line_reporter'
include CommandLineReporter

puts 'Please input the FQDN of the node your interested in:'
fqdn = gets.chomp

uri = URI.parse('http://localhost:8080/v3/facts/')URI.parse('http://
localhost:8080/v3/facts/')
params = {:query => '["=", "certname",' + '"' "#{fqdn}" + '"' ']'}
uri.query = URI.encode_www_form(params)

          response = Net::HTTP.get_response(uri)
          json = JSON.parse(response.body)

table(:border => true) do
          json.each do |fact|
          row do
          column(fact['name'], :width => 20)
          column(fact['value'], :width => 60, :align => 'right',
            :padding => 5)
          end
   end
end
```

Go ahead and run the program. After entering a **fully qualified domain name (FQDN)** that matches one of your Puppet client certificates, you should have an output that looks a little like what's shown in the following screenshot:

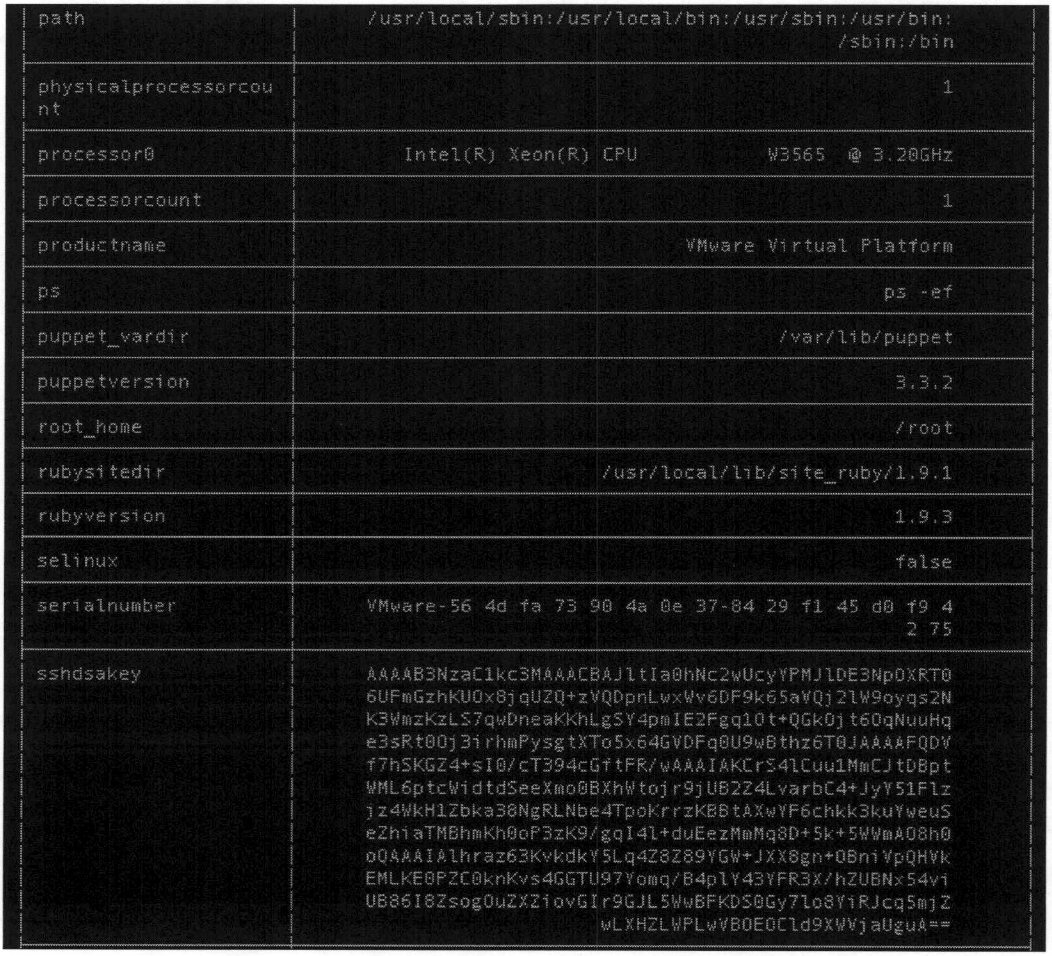

path	/usr/local/sbin:/usr/local/bin:/usr/sbin:/usr/bin:/sbin:/bin
physicalprocessorcount	1
processor0	Intel(R) Xeon(R) CPU W3565 @ 3.20GHz
processorcount	1
productname	VMware Virtual Platform
ps	ps -ef
puppet_vardir	/var/lib/puppet
puppetversion	3.3.2
root_home	/root
rubysitedir	/usr/local/lib/site_ruby/1.9.1
rubyversion	1.9.3
selinux	false
serialnumber	VMware-56 4d fa 73 90 4a 0e 37-84 29 f1 45 d0 f9 42 75
sshdsakey	AAAAB3NzaC1kc3MAAACBAJ1tIa0hNc2wUcyYPMJlDE3NpOXRT06UFmGzhKU0x8jqUZQ+zVQDpnLwxWv6DF9k65aVQj2lW9oyqs2NK3WmzKzLS7qwDneaKKhLgSY4pmIE2Fgq10t+QGk0jt60qNuuHqe3sRt00j3irhmPysgtXTo5x64GVDFq0U9wBthz6T0JAAAAFQDVf7hSKGZ4+sI0/cT394cGftFR/wAAAIAKCrS41Cuu1MmCJtDBptWML6ptcWidtdSeeXmo0BXhWtojr9jUB2Z4LvarbC4+JyY51Flzjz4WkH1Zbka38NgRLNbe4TpoKrrzKBBtAXwYF6chkk3kuYweuSeZhiaTMBhmKh0oF3zK9/gqI4l+duEezMmMq8D+5k+5WWmA08h0oQAAAIAlhraz63KvkdkY5Lq4Z8Z89YGW+JXX8gn+0BniVpQHVkEMLKE0PZC0knKvs4GGTU97Yomq/B4plY43YFR3X/hZUBNx54viUB86I8Zsog0uZXZiovGIr9GJL5WwBFKDS0Gy7lo8YiRJcq5mjZwLXHZLWPLwVBOEOCld9XWVjaUguA==

This is an excellent, albeit somewhat limited example of what we can do with the PuppetDB API, and it should give you an idea of how to work with the data it provides. Now that we are comfortable with the fundamentals of how to communicate with PuppetDB, we can take a look at something a little more sophisticated. Let's look at how we can create a relatively simple application that can give users the ability to query both for hardware details and a summary of the last Puppet client run.

Creating a menu-driven PuppetDB application

As we're designing this query application for nontechnical users, we want a way for them to interact with our application without needing to deal with esoteric command-line options. This is a command-line application; therefore, fancy GUIs and shiny web applications are right out. Instead, we have to go back to the tried and tested system of using a menu-driven application. However, first of all, let's figure out what we want this application to do.

One of the more common scenarios where you might want to offer this type of application is for anyone who is interested in, works with, or is auditing your Puppet-managed infrastructure. You might not want them to have full and free access to your Puppet installation, but at the same time, you want them to be able to find the information they need to carry out the task at hand. So, the first decision that we need to make is regarding the information that we give them access to. For this application, we're going to offer the following information:

- Summary of the last Puppet run
- Hardware specifications of a particular node
- Details of what, if anything, Puppet changed in the last run

This should give our users enough access to the PuppetDB information to allow them to answer any basic questions they may have.

Setting up the UI

We're going to create the code in discrete chunks, with separate functions for presenting the menu, collecting the hardware details, and outputting the Puppet report. This not only helps us keep our code nice and tidy and encourages reuse, but it also makes it easy to extend our application by simply dropping in new modules. This is a technique worth using for anything more than a simple twenty-line application. Many a sensible developer or DevOps engineer has been reduced to bitter tears of frustration when they are asked to support a five thousand-line piece of spaghetti coding with no discernible entry points for a given function.

The first task that we're going to tackle is creating the menu for our user to interact with. To make this easy, we're going to use a gem called HighLine. HighLine makes it very simple to construct interactive command-line applications and includes powerful features such as validation, masked input, and type conversion without the tedious messing around with the `gets()` and `puts()` functions. Using HighLine, we can quickly and easily create the basic UI our users are going to interact with. Go ahead and create a new folder called `puppetreport`; this is where we're going to place our code. Also, create a file called `puppetreport.rb` using your favorite editor. Once you are done, insert the following code in that file:

```
require 'highline/import'
require 'json'
require 'net/http'
require 'uri'
require 'command_line_reporter'

require_relative 'hwdetails.rb'
require_relative 'rundetails.rb'

@puppetdb = 'http://localhost:8080'


loop do
  choose do |menu|

  menu.choice('Enter Host') do |command|
    @fqdn = ask('Please enter FQDN')
  end

  menu.choice('Hardware Details') do |command|
    if @fqdn then
      get_hw_details
    else
      @fqdn = ask('Please enter FQDN')
    end
  end

  menu.choice('Result of last Puppet Run') do |command|
    if @fqdn then
      get_run_details
    else
      @fqdn = ask('Please enter FQDN')
    end
```

```
    end

    menu.choice('Exit program.') { exit }
    end
  end
```

This small chunk of code creates the user menu. We're giving the user four actions to choose from here: to enter the fully qualified domain name of a host to query, a hardware listing for that host, details of the Puppet run, and finally, a way to exit the program.

You will recognize the first five lines as code to include the libraries that we require to interact with PuppetDB, parse its response, and create a nice-looking output using the `command_line_reporter` library. We also have a newcomer in the shape of the `highline/import` library requirement; this is used to include the HighLine library into our application. You'll notice almost straightaway that the `puppetreport.rb` file doesn't make use of any of the libraries, except for the `highline/import` library. As you can see after the library `require` statements, we're also requesting two more Ruby files, which are `hwdetails.rb` and `rundetails.rb`. These two files will be created next and will contain the code that will make use of the other libraries. We're going to cover these files in later sections, but for the moment, let's explore the code that creates our user interface.

After the library `require` statements, we set our one and only option. This is described in the following line of code:

```
@puppetdb = 'http://localhost:8080'
```

To keep the application simple, I've left this as a hardcoded variable, but it would be easy enough to read this from a file. Note the `@` symbol; in Ruby, this denotes an instance variable. An instance variable is scope confined to the owning object; in this case, this is our application. If this were defined as a local variable (a variable that begins with a lowercase letter or the _ character), then it would be inaccessible from our new functions.

Now to the menu! Firstly, we want to make sure that when users launch the application, they don't just choose one option and have the application closed after finishing the output. Even with the various command recall functions in the bash shell, this is going to get old very quickly. Instead, we use a loop to ensure that the user is returned to the menu after each interaction. We then create a Ruby block to iterate through our menu choices. This is described in the following code snippet:

```
loop do
  choose do |menu|

  menu.choice('Enter Host') do |command|
```

```
    @fqdn = ask('Please enter FQDN')
  end
```

As you can see, the `choice` function allows you to enter the text to be presented to the user and then the command that you want to run. In the case of the first option, this is a simple prompt for the user to enter the fully qualified domain name of the host they are interested in, and the next three menu choices are much the same. This is described in the following code snippet:

```
  menu.choice('Enter Host') do |command|
    @fqdn = ask('Please enter FQDN')
  end

  menu.choice('Hardware Details') do |command|
    if @fqdn then
      get_hw_details
    else
      @fqdn = ask('Please enter FQDN')
    end
  end

  menu.choice('Result of last Puppet Run') do |command|
    if @fqdn then
      get_run_details
    else
      @fqdn = ask('Please enter FQDN')
    end
  end

  menu.choice('Exit program.') { exit }
  end
```

Each of the choices resemble the first choice in terms of their overall structure; however, in the case of the hardware details and details of the Puppet run, we're also applying a little bit of logic to ensure that if users have skipped over entering a host, we prompt them so that an FQDN is entered. Note the two function calls: `get_hw_details` and `get_run_details`. These are the two methods that we're about to create to allow us to pull data from PuppetDB. Let's start with the simpler of the two, the facts lookup.

Querying PuppetDB's facts endpoint

The first function that we're going to create is going to go to PuppetDB, which is configured in the `puppetreport.rb` file, and interrogate the `facts` endpoint for information about the user-specified host. We're then going to make use of the `command_line_reporter` library to ensure that the output is easily readable to our users. Go ahead and create a new file in the `puppetreport` directory called `hwdetails.rb`, and open it with your favorite editor.

The first few lines of our application deal with creating our new method, setting out what URLs to query, and then connecting to PuppetDB and fetching a response. Take a look at the following code snippet:

```
def get_hw_details

  include CommandLineReporter

  uri = URI.parse("#{@puppetdb}/v3/facts/")
  params = {:query => '["=", "certname",' + '"' "#{@fqdn}" + '"' ']'}
  uri.query = URI.encode_www_form(params)

  begin
  response = Net::HTTP.get_response(uri)
  rescue StandardError
    puts 'PuppetDB is currently unavailable'
    exit
  end

  json = JSON.parse(response.body)
```

The first line creates our method in the usual manner using the `def` keyword. Next, we include our `CommandLineReporter` library so that it's ready for use, and then we go into the connectivity activities. Firstly, we create a variable called `uri` to hold our PuppetDB connection details; this is constructed using the instance variable we defined in the `puppetreport.rb` file and points at v3 of the `facts` endpoint. Next, we construct our query and assign it to the `params` variable; note again the string interpolation that inserts the FQDN of the client based on the input that the user provided when entering the application. Finally, we call the `uri.query` method to take the `params` variable and encode it as an HTTP query string.

That's all the ground work for the PuppetDB connection out of the way; all that's required now is to attempt the connection using the `Net::HTTP` library. As you can see, I've wrapped this in a `begin` and `rescue` construct. This application is aimed at nontechnical or semi-technical users, so we want to try and make the application fail gracefully. In this case, we are rescuing anything that arrives via `StandardError`; this should cover pretty much any issues that the `Net::HTTP` library will encounter and will give the users an error message to inform them that PuppetDB is not currently available. We then exit the application, as it's of extremely limited use if there is no PuppetDB to supply it with data.

Outputting the hardware report

Assuming that all went well and we were able to connect to PuppetDB, our `response` variable should now have the response from PuppetDB's `facts` endpoint in the JSON format. As parsing JSON by hand is incredibly dull, we're going to make use of the `JSON` library to do the heavy lifting for us. We're assigning the output of the `JSON.parse` method to a variable called `json`, and this should give us a nicely formatted array of JSON data to process in the next step.

Now that we have the data, we need to process it. By default, the `facts` endpoint returns the data in a JSON object, and this contains a list of key values made up of fact names. The outputted JSON file in v3 of the Puppet API looks like the following code snippet:

```
{"name": "<node>",
 "facts": {
     "<fact name>": "<fact value>",
     "<fact name>": "<fact value>",
     ...
    }
}
```

There are several different techniques you could use to work with this data, but in this case, we're going to create a new instance variable called `@facts` and then use a simple Ruby block to iterate over our data and insert it into our newly created hash. This is described in the following code snippet:

```
json = JSON.parse(response.body)
@facts = Hash.new

json.each do |fact|
    @facts[fact['name']] = fact['value']
end
```

As you can see from the preceding example, you only need a little code to extract data from the PuppetDB API. Let's go ahead and output the data for our user; remember, we're going to use the `CommandLineReporter` library to make the output easy to read. For this application, we're going to give the user three different sections of data about the hardware, a section of summary facts (memory, CPU details, and so on), a section on the BIOS details, and finally, some details about the main board. We'll present these details as three separate tables to make them easier to read. Add the following code to the `hwdetails.rb` file:

```
system "clear" or system "cls"
  header :title => "Hardware report for #{@fqdn}", :width => 80,
    :align => 'center', :rule => true, :color => 'green', :bold =>
    true, :timestamp => true

  table(:border => true) do
    row do
      column('manufacturer', :width => 30)
      column("#{@facts["manufacturer"]}", :width => 40)
    end
    row do
      column('productname', :width => 30)
      column("#{@facts["productname"]}", :width => 40)
    end
    row do
      column('Number of processors', :width => 30)
      column("#{@facts["physicalprocessorcount"]}", :width => 40)
    end
    row do
      column('Memory', :width => 30)
      column("#{@facts["memorysize"]}", :width => 40)
    end
    row do
      column('architecture', :width => 30)
      column("#{@facts["architecture"]}", :width => 40)
    end
    row do
      column('Virtualized?', :width => 30)
      column("#{@facts["is_virtual"]}", :width => 40)
    end

  end
```

The first line of the code is used to call out the `clear` command on the system; this is essentially the same as typing `clear` or `cls` on the command line and ensures that our users will not have any clutter on their screen to distract them. Next, we output a header to remind the users what the report is about. As you can see in this code, the `header` method of the `command_line_reporter` library accepts a broad range of options to allow you to style it, and in our case, we've asked for it to be 80 characters wide, aligned to the center of the screen with green underlined text, with a timestamp of when the command was issued. It'll look something like what is shown in the following screenshot:

```
              Hardware report for puppetagent.localhost
                     2014-03-17 - 10:36:24PM
```

Once we've shown the user the header, we go right ahead and create our first table. This table is going to be used to contain the general hardware details, but rather than simply spewing out all of the data that the `facts` endpoint produces, we're going to be selective and give our users details that are relevant to the query. In this case, we're going to show them the following details:

- The manufacturer
- The product name
- The number of processors
- The memory size
- The processor architecture
- The virtual machine flag

As you can see in the preceding code, we define the data by row, and within each row, we specify a number of columns. Our first column is a simple text label with a width of 30 characters. The next column contains the data to match that label and is taken from the hash we created and populated with the data from the `facts` endpoint. This is described in the following code snippet:

```
row do
  column('manufacturer', :width => 30)
  column("#{@facts["manufacturer"]}", :width => 40)
end
```

Let's go ahead and add the rest of our details. This is described in the following code:

```
row do
  column('productname', :width => 30)
```

```
    column("#{@facts["productname"]}", :width => 40)
  end

  row do
    column('Number of processors', :width => 30)
    column("#{@facts["physicalprocessorcount"]}", :width => 40)
  end
  row do
    column('Memory', :width => 30)
    column("#{@facts["memorysize"]}", :width => 40)
  end
  row do
    column('architecture', :width => 30)
    column("#{@facts["architecture"]}", :width => 40)
  end
  row do
    column('Virtualized?', :width => 30)
    column("#{@facts["is_virtual"]}", :width => 40)
  end
```

This is a good start for our hardware report, and if you were to run this code now, you'd be able to retrieve some relevant data. We have got a few more pieces of information that will be of interest to the user, though, such as the BIOS details and motherboard details; this, in particular, is a good piece of data to output as it has the serial number on it. We want to keep the output easy to read, though, so the first thing we do is put a thin line underneath the previous output to denote that we're moving onto a different set of data. This is described in the following code:

```
horizontal_rule :width => 70, :color => 'red'
vertical_spacing 1
header :title => 'Bios Details'
```

Again, we have several formatting options, but we're going to keep it simple and understated, and simply put a red line across the screen and add a header underneath. Now, we simply have to add the rest of our data. This is described in the following code:

```
table(:border => true) do
  row do
    column('Bios release date', :width => 30)
    column("#{@facts["bios_release_date"]}", :width => 40)
  end
  row do
    column('Bios Vendor', :width => 30)
    column("#{@facts["bios_vendor"]}", :width => 40)
```

```
      end
      row do
        column('Bios Version', :width => 30)
        column("#{@facts["bios_version"]}", :width => 40)
      end
    end

  horizontal_rule :width => 70, :color => 'red'
  vertical_spacing 1
  header :title => 'Motherboard Details'

    table(:border => true) do
      row do
        column('Motherboard Manufacturer', :width => 30)
        column("#{@facts["boardmanufacturer"]}", :width => 40)
      end
      row do
        column('Motherboard Name', :width => 30)
        column("#{@facts["boardproductname"]}", :width => 40)
      end
      row do
        column('Motherboard Serial number', :width => 30)
        column("#{@facts["boardserialnumber"]}", :width => 40)
      end
    end

  end
```

Fantastic! We now have a simple but very effective tool to query hardware data held in PuppetDB. We could leave it there, but one of the questions that I find is asked quite often by clients with Puppet-managed nodes is, "What has Puppet done to my server?" This is a fair question, so let's give our users a way to query it.

Querying PuppetDB for report information

Essentially, we're going to use the same techniques that we learned in the previous examples, but the way we process the data is going to change. One thing you'll almost immediately notice is that each endpoint has its own particular format; although they all return JSON output, sometimes, it's a JSON array, other times, a flat JSON document, and so on. When working with PuppetDB, it's worth reviewing the documentation for the endpoints, as it contains an excellent rundown of what to expect. Again, you can find the documentation at `https://docs.puppetlabs.com/puppetdb/latest/`.

> One tool that can be enormously helpful when exploring data such as the PuppetDB API is the pp library that ships with Ruby. The pp library is the pretty printer for Ruby and will take data such as JSON and output it in a reasonably clear way. This can be a real help if you are not sure how or what data is going to be returned. If you get stuck, remember that you can use the puts <variable> class to discover if you've been passed an array, hash, or some other data type.

The get_run_details method is going to be slightly more complex than the previous method we created. This is because we are going to blend the information from three different endpoints to generate this report. These are the reports endpoint, event-counts endpoint, and finally, the events endpoint. This allows us to do several things. First and most importantly, it allows us to find the hash of the last Puppet report; this is vital as it's the connection between the report and the events. It also allows us to quickly count how many event types we had without resorting to manually counting them ourselves, and finally, it gives us the details of what happened to the node when Puppet was run on it last time. When we're finished, it's going to look like the following screenshot:

```
                    2014-03-17 - 10:54:07PM

| Failures | Successes | Noops | Skips |
| 0        | 1         | 0     | 0     |

Event Details

| Resource Title      | rvm_version                              |
| Resource Type       | Notify                                   |
| Property            | message                                  |
| Old Value           | absent                                   |
| New Value           | RVM version 1.23.14                      |
| Status              | success                                  |
| Event Date and Time | 2014-03-03T23:20:22.223Z                 |
| Message             | defined 'message' as 'RVM version 1.23.14' |
|                     |                                          |
```

Creating the PuppetDB query method

Let's start by creating a file for our new method. Remember, it's generally tidier to split large pieces of code into their own file, as this keeps the application tidy and makes it more obvious where you can find the functionality. Create a new file in the `puppetreport` directory, called `rundetails.rb`, and open it up in your editor. We're going to start in the usual way and define the name of our method using the `def` keyword and then connect to each of our endpoints and retrieve our details. First up, we have the `reports` endpoint. Consider the following code:

```
def get_run_details

  include CommandLineReporter

  reporturi = URI.parse("#{@puppetdb}/v3/reports/")
  reportparams = {:query => '["=", "certname",' + '"' "#{@fqdn}" +
    '"' ']'}
  reporturi.query = URI.encode_www_form(reportparams)

  reportresponse = Net::HTTP.get_response(reporturi)
  reportjson = JSON.parse(reportresponse.body)
  report = reportjson.last
```

As you can see, this looks very similar to the way we connected to the `facts` endpoint, and again, we are taking the instance variable that contains the PuppetDB location and are using it to construct our URL. We're then constructing a PuppetDB query based around the FQDN that the users have given as input when they launched the application; the main thing to note in this code is the use of the `.last` method when we assign the value of the retrieved JSON file. This report is specifically for the last report that Puppet ran; we don't need any others. As the `reports` endpoint is returning an array of reports, we can use the `.last` method to simply retrieve the last one without needing to mess around iterating through the array ourselves.

Fetching the event counts

Now that we have the report summary, we need to go and get our event counts; this is exactly what the `event-counts` endpoint was designed for, to save calculating the count ourselves. We connect to this endpoint and retrieve the data in much the same way as the other endpoints. This is described in the following code:

```
ecounturi = URI.parse("#{@puppetdb}/v3/event-counts")
ecountparams = {'query' => '["=", "report",' + '"'
  "#{report["hash"]}" + '"' ']', 'summarize-by' => "certname"}
```

```
ecounturi.query = URI.encode_www_form(ecountparams)

ecountresponse = Net::HTTP.get_response(ecounturi)
ecountjson = JSON.parse(ecountresponse.body).first
```

There are two things to note in this chunk of code. Firstly, take a look at the query we're constructing. This time, rather than using the FQDN that the user has given as input, we're taking the value of the `hash` field from the Puppet report we assigned to the `report` variable. The hash is our key to get to any event data generated by Puppet and ensures that you're only looking at data for that particular Puppet run. The second thing to note is the use of the `.first` method when accessing the data. The `event-counts` endpoint returns an array of hashes; however, in our case, because we are asking for a specific hash, we should only ever return an array with a single member. Using the `.first` method is a nice and simple shorthand to return that single piece of data without needing to work with the array ourselves.

The final piece of information we need to retrieve is the events themselves. Again, we're going to construct our connection details, connect to PuppetDB, and use a query that contains the report hash to retrieve the data we're interested in. This is described in the following query:

```
eventsuri = URI.parse("#{@puppetdb}/v3/events")
eventsparams = {'query' => '["=", "report",' + '"' "#{report["hash"]}"
+ '"' ']'}
eventsuri.query = URI.encode_www_form(eventsparams)

eventsresponse = Net::HTTP.get_response(eventsuri)
eventsjson = JSON.parse(eventsresponse.body)
```

Presenting the events data

The `events` endpoint returns its data in the form of an array of events. We need the whole of the array, so we'll process them at the output time rather than doing anything here. Now that we have our data, we can go ahead and output it. Again, we're going to use tables to output the data to make it easily readable. Let's start by giving our user a summary of the report data. Consider the following code:

```
system 'clear'

header :title => "Puppet run report for #{@fqdn}", :width => 80,
  :align => 'center', :rule => true, :color => 'green', :bold =>
  true, :timestamp => true

  table(:border => true) do
```

```
    row do
      column('Failures', :width => 10)
      column('Successes', :width => 10)
      column('Noops', :width => 10)
      column('Skips', :width => 10)
    end

    row do
      column("#{ecountjson["failures"]}", :width => 10)
      column("#{ecountjson["successes"]}", :width => 10)
      column("#{ecountjson["noops"]}", :width => 10)
      column("#{ecountjson["skips"]}", :width => 10)
    end

  end
```

We start by clearing the screen. When producing applications that report on the command line, it's pretty essential that we do this; otherwise, the screen soon becomes cluttered and unreadable. Next, we're outputting a header to let the user know which host this report was generated from, and we're also applying some formatting to make it stand out. We then take the data that we've created and output it into a table.

The table format is slightly different this time around, and that's because rather than having the data alongside the heading, I've used the more traditional columnar data format. It's a little more readable for this kind of data. We're using keys to access the hash data that was retrieved from the `event-counts` endpoint. When you are looking at a host, one of the first things that we should check is how many resources were applied and likewise, how many failed.

> If you're an experienced coder, then you might have noticed a way to improve this application. As we already have the event data, we could potentially gather our event counts while gathering the events rather than going to the `event-counts` endpoint. This would work for this application, but it's worth knowing how to use it for applications where it would be more efficient to use the `event-counts` endpoint. Certainly, if you are not gathering event data, you would have to go back to the `event-counts` endpoint for this data.

Now that we've got the counts of the events, let's move on and let our user see what actions those events performed. Again, we're going to add a subheader to mark out the new section, and we're then going to use the data we gathered from the `events` endpoint to add the data. This is described in the following code:

```
horizontal_rule :width => 70, :color => 'red'
vertical_spacing 1
```

```
header :title => 'Event Details'

  table(:border => true) do
    eventsjson.each do |event|

      row do
        column('Resource Title', :width => 20)
        column(event['resource-title'], :width => 60)
      end

      row do
        column('Resource Type', :width => 20)
        column(event['resource-type'], :width => 60)
      end

      row do
        column('Property', :width => 20)
        column(event['property'], :width => 60)
      end

      row do
        column('Old Value', :width => 20)
        column(event['old-value'], :width => 60)
      end

      row do
        column('New Value', :width => 20)
        column(event['new-value'], :width => 60)
      end

      row do
        column('Status', :width => 20)
        column(event['status'], :width => 60)
      end

      row do
        column('Event Date and Time', :width => 20)
        column(event['timestamp'], :width => 60)
      end

      row do
        column('Message', :width => 20)
        column(event['message'], :width => 60)
```

```
        end

        row do
          column('', :width => 80)
        end

      end
    end
  end
```

This should be fairly familiar to you by now. Again, we've used the `horizontal_rule` method to output a nicely formatted section break, and we're also creating a new table. We are then using a Ruby block to iterate through the array of data contained in the JSON response from the `events` endpoint. Each iteration takes the next piece of data and feeds it into a hash called `event`, and this then allows us to output the data using its hash key. Again, we're being selective; although there is more data available, we're focusing on the data that is relevant to this report rather than outputting it all.

Testing our application

We now have a small yet very functional reporting application that uses PuppetDB as its data source. Let's go ahead and run it by opening a shell in our `puppetreport` directory and running the following command:

`rubypuppetreport.rb`

You should be presented with a menu, as shown in the following screenshot:

```
1. Enter Host
2. Hardware Details
3. Result of last Puppet Run
4. Exit program.
?
```

Let's go ahead and add our host, either by selecting the first option or by selecting another option and being prompted to enter a host. Next, let's take a look at its hardware details; you should have a report that looks something like what is shown in the following screenshot:

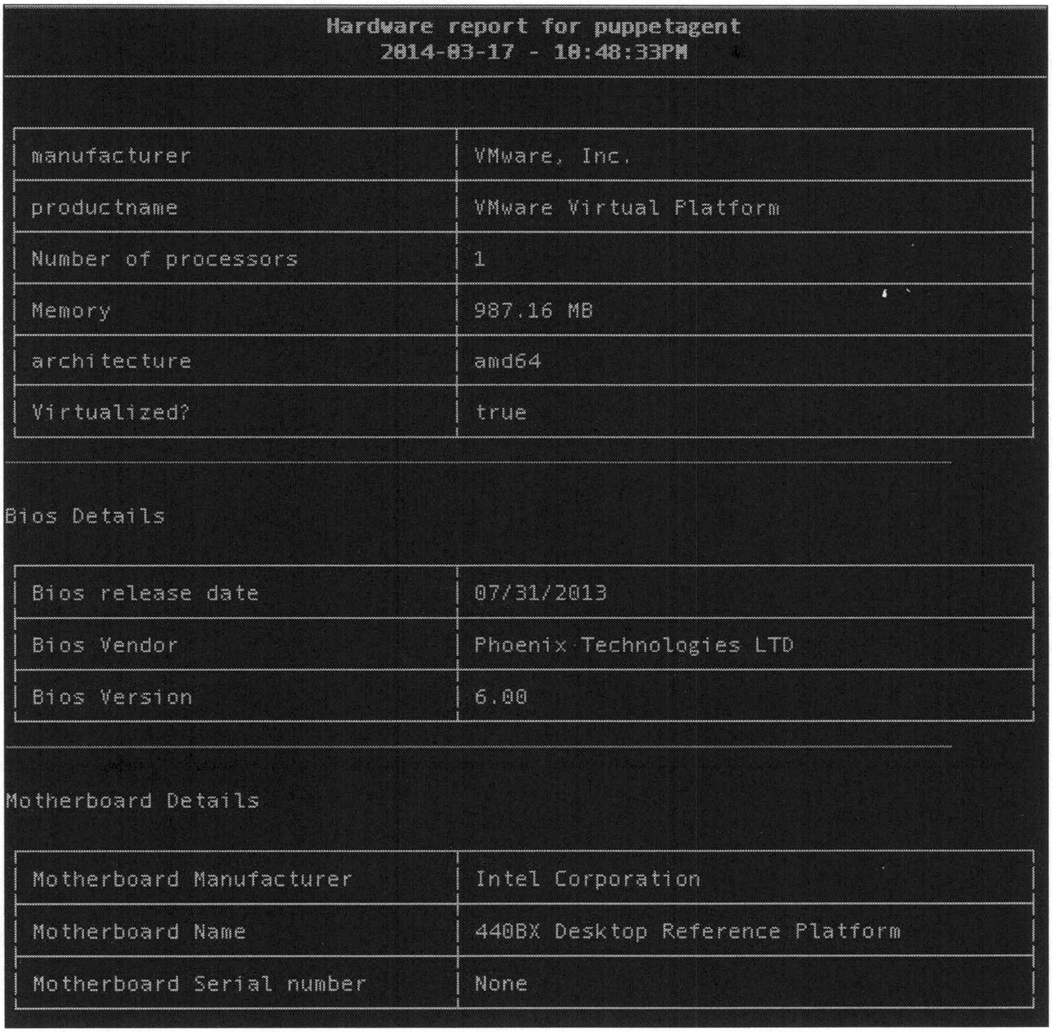

Hardware report for puppetagent
2014-03-17 - 10:48:33PM

manufacturer	VMware, Inc.
productname	VMware Virtual Platform
Number of processors	1
Memory	987.16 MB
architecture	amd64
Virtualized?	true

Bios Details

Bios release date	07/31/2013
Bios Vendor	Phoenix Technologies LTD
Bios Version	6.00

Motherboard Details

Motherboard Manufacturer	Intel Corporation
Motherboard Name	440BX Desktop Reference Platform
Motherboard Serial number	None

That looks rather splendid! Finally, let's take a look at the changes that Puppet did to this server during the last Puppet run by selecting the third option. This can be seen in the following screenshot:

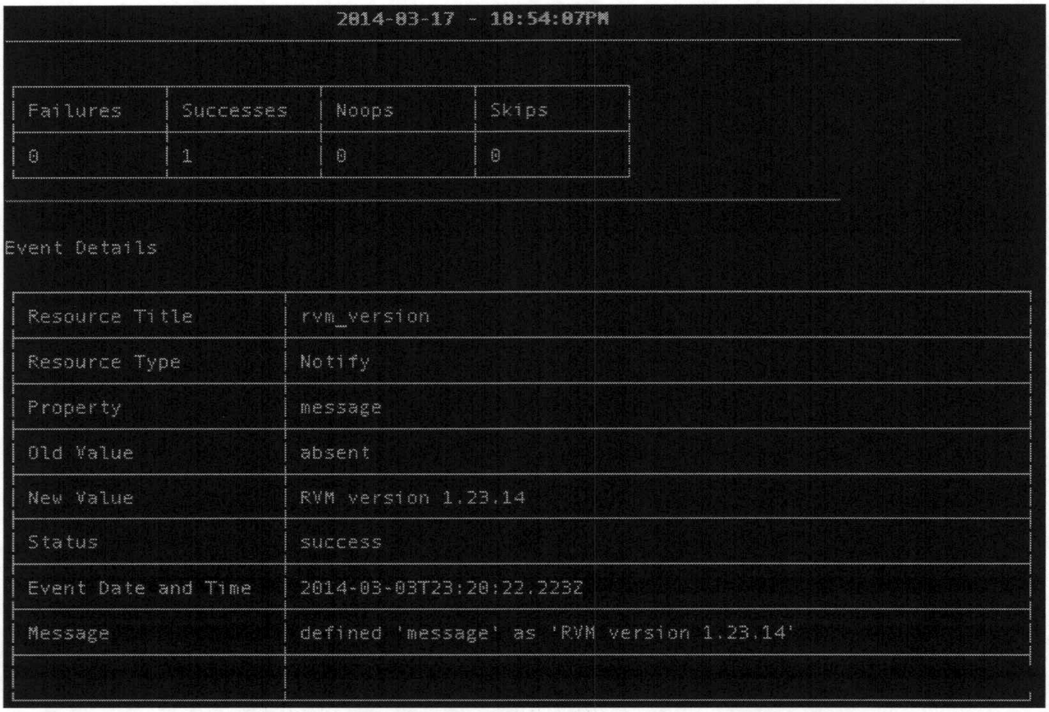

2014-03-17 - 18:54:07PM

Failures	Successes	Noops	Skips
0	1	0	0

Event Details

Resource Title	rvm_version
Resource Type	Notify
Property	message
Old Value	absent
New Value	RVM version 1.23.14
Status	success
Event Date and Time	2014-03-03T23:20:22.223Z
Message	defined 'message' as 'RVM version 1.23.14'

We can now hand this on to our users and let them merrily query PuppetDB without needing to mess around with the `curl` statements or constructing complex queries.

As you can see, working with the PuppetDB data is relatively straightforward, and although the application we created in this chapter is extremely simple, it exposes a surprising amount of data, and this is just scratching the surface. By exploring the data available within PuppetDB, you can easily use Ruby, Python, Java, or any other programming language to create rich portals into this information. As long as you can parse the JSON output, you have access to a wealth of detail about your infrastructure. It's well worth playing around and extending this code, both to increase the utility of the application and also as a way to explore the data. For example, adding in another function that creates a summary of all your managed files would be reasonably simple using the `catalogs` endpoint.

Summary

We've covered a lot of ground in this chapter and worked on some exciting and very useful techniques to work with PuppetDB. In this chapter, we've taken a look at how we can create a simple Ruby application to extract details of the hardware, reports, and events from PuppetDB and used some freely available libraries to ensure that our output looks elegant and readable. By creating this application, we've learned that although PuppetDB returns JSON as its format, the actual layout of the JSON feed may vary, and we've looked at various ways in which we can work with some of that data.

In the next chapter, we will look at ways to create our own custom dashboard to present PuppetDB data in an easy-to-use and attractive form using freely available open source software.

8 Creating Your Own Custom Dashboard

Over the past few chapters, we've looked at the many ways in which you can both gather and present data from Puppet. We have also created custom alerts and applications for our users to gather their own information with. But we're still reliant on the dashboards that we looked at in *Chapter 2, Viewing Data in Dashboards*. That's not to say that they aren't any good, but the trouble with a pre-made solution is that it might not do exactly what you'd like.

In this chapter, we're going to create our own dashboard using PuppetDB as the data source and combine it with an open source framework for creating dashboards called **Dashing**. We're going to learn the following topics:

- What Dashing is and what it can be used for
- How to create Dashing jobs
- How to integrate PuppetDB data into Dashing
- How to make Dashing react to data

At the end of this chapter, you should have a functional and good-looking dashboard that quickly imparts some key facts to anyone who happens to be glancing at it.

Exploring Dashing

Dashing is a framework for creating reporting dashboards quickly, easily, and with minimal understanding of frontend development. Under the hood, it uses the **Sinatra** framework to deal with the servicing of incoming web requests and uses Ruby for backend data processing, with a language called CoffeeScript dealing with the frontend.

> Sinatra is a framework for creating web applications in Ruby and is similar to the well-known Ruby on Rails project. Unlike the more fully-featured Ruby on Rails, Sinatra focuses on providing a very lightweight framework that allows you to use mostly plain old Ruby to develop your application; this is in contrast to Ruby on Rails, which also provides a more rigid framework but a far more extensive set of features.

You can download Dashing from `http://shopify.github.io/dashing/`. At present, it hasn't got an extensive set of documentation, but you can find some good additional details on the project's wiki page at `https://github.com/Shopify/dashing/wiki`. As you'll see later in this chapter, it ships with some example dashboards that you can examine for more clues as to how it works.

Dashing has been released as an open source product by the developers behind **Shopify** (`http://www.shopify.com`), and it is part of a growing trend of companies allowing developers to create and release software that are not core products as open source. Other companies such as Etsy and Netflix have also opened up some of their internally-used software as open source products, and from the perspective of the DevOps community at large, this is a fantastic addition to the community.

Dashing uses the idea of widgets to display data, with each widget potentially showing a different dataset in a different way. Dashing ships with a number of pre-made widgets that can deal with anything from text presentation to building graphs, and a fair bit besides. Dashing has adopted a visual style similar to Microsoft's Windows 8 tiles, and the simple and flat look allows data to be easily digested and understood. Take a look at the following example dashboard:

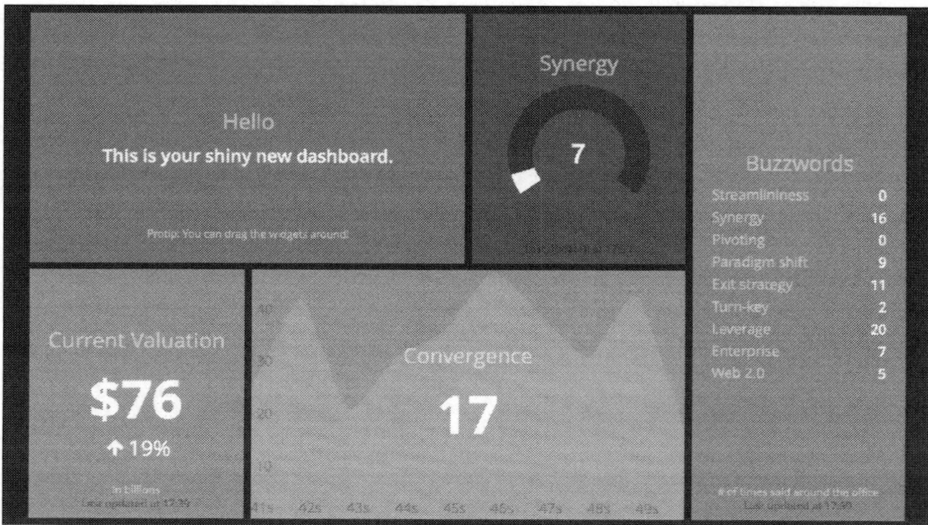

You can check out this dashboard at `http://dashingdemo.herokuapp.com/sample`. The first thing that you will notice if you open it in a browser is that it immediately draws the eye with motion, as several of the widgets update and reflect changes by either moving the swing meter around or pushing the graph along. This is more than just a static display of data, and Dashing makes understated effects such as the dial sweep and graph animation very simple to implement.

So how does Dashing fit with Puppet? As it turns out, very well. There is a huge amount of data generated by Puppet, and although the dashboards that are freely available are excellent, they are also focused on in-depth data exploration rather than reading the status at a glance. Puppet Dashboard, Puppet Enterprise Console, and The Foreman are all geared to be used as **External Node Classifiers** (**ENC**), and so the GUI is set for not only interacting with data, but also for acting on it. PuppetBoard is used for reporting, but is focused on exploration of data; you can spend many happy hours drilling into nodes to find out the many details that Puppet Dashboard contains, but you can't really glance at it and see the state of your infrastructure.

Using Dashing, we are able to produce a dashboard that provides non-Puppet-focused users, such as developers or support personnel, a window into what Puppet is doing at any given time, and it gives them the ability to very quickly see the data that's important to them. When we're done, our dashboard is going to look as shown in the following screenshot:

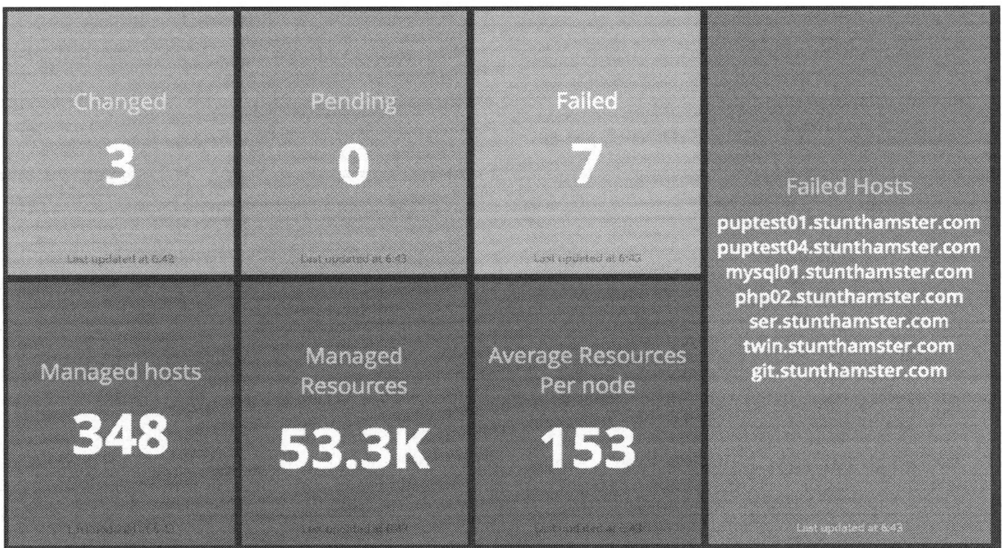

As you can see, we're presenting some basic but important facts about what Puppet has changed, and we're also adding in some fun statistics, such as the number of managed resources and the last host that applied changes. That's a lot of information in a single screen, and it's all formatted so you can take it all in at a glance.

Setting up Dashing

Dashing is very simple to install and keep updated using the RubyGems package management system. To install Dashing, simply follow these steps:

1. Enter the following command in your command prompt:

   ```
   gem install dashing
   ```

2. Once it's installed, we can go straight ahead and create our dashboard. Dashing has a built-in function to create a skeleton application for us to work with and will also give you some example code to look at. Navigate to your `projects` folder and issue the following command:

   ```
   dashing new puppetdash
   ```

3. After running the command, you should have a new directory called `puppetdash`, which contains your new skeleton application. We now only have to complete one more step, which is to instruct the Bundler package manager to download and install the required libraries for Bundler. Ensure that you're in the root of your new project and then issue the following command:

   ```
   bundle install
   ```

This command looks inside the `gem` file that was created along with the rest of the project and will then use the Bundler package manager to install any missing libraries that Dashing requires. Be warned: Dashing has quite an extensive set of requirements, so expect to see quite a few additional gems installed.

Exploring the default puppetdash directory layout

Let's change directories and go to the `puppetdash` directory and look at what files have been created for us. You should find a directory listing as shown in the following screenshot:

```
drwxr-xr-x  11 staff  374 21 Mar 07:13 widgets
drwxr-xr-x   4 staff  136 21 Mar 07:13 public
drwxr-xr-x   2 staff   68 21 Mar 07:13 lib
drwxr-xr-x   8 staff  272 24 Mar 06:15 jobs
drwxr-xr-x   6 staff  204 23 Mar 22:18 dashboards
-rw-r--r--   1 staff  339 21 Mar 07:13 config.ru
drwxr-xr-x   6 staff  204 21 Mar 07:13 assets
-rw-r--r--   1 staff   65 21 Mar 07:13 README.md
-rw-r--r--   1 staff  122 21 Mar 07:13 Gemfile
```

Each of the directories inside the Dashing application serve a particular purpose, so let's quickly run through them and see what they are:

- `widgets`: This directory holds the Dashing widget code. Widgets are made up of directories containing CoffeeScript, HTML, and **Syntactically Awesome Style Sheets** (**SASS**) style sheets. This is where you would create any new widgets or place any of the third-party widgets that are available.
- `public`: This folder is a standard Sinatra folder and is used to host any static files. Within Dashing, this is used for the "404 page not found" HTML and browser favicon.
- `lib`: This is another standard Sinatra folder. At the time of writing, Dashing isn't using this, but this is generally where external libraries required for the application will be stored. If you heavily customize Dashing, you might find that you will need to use this in the future.
- `jobs`: This folder is where we are going to be spending most of our time in this chapter. Jobs are the mechanism that Dashing uses to import data into its various dashboards, and these are simple pieces of Ruby code that fetch information and use the `send_event` function to send the data to a receiving widget (or set of widgets).
- `assets`: This folder is used to contain the various images, JavaScript codes, and fonts that Dashing uses. It's here that you will find the core JavaScript libraries that Dashing uses to construct its grid layout, animation, and basic styling.
- `dashboards`: The `dashboards` folder is where the files that make up the actual dashboards are stored. Dashboards are created using the embedded Ruby templating language (ERB) to define the layout. We'll look at this in a bit more detail when we create our own dashboard.

Running Dashing

Now that we know where everything is kept, let's go ahead and start Dashing and see how it looks in its default shipping state. Open a new terminal session at the root of the `puppetdash` folder and issue the following command:

```
dashing start
```

This will start the Dashing application and have it listen on the local host, port 3030. Open your browser and go to `http://localhost:3030`. You should be greeted with a page that looks like the following screenshot:

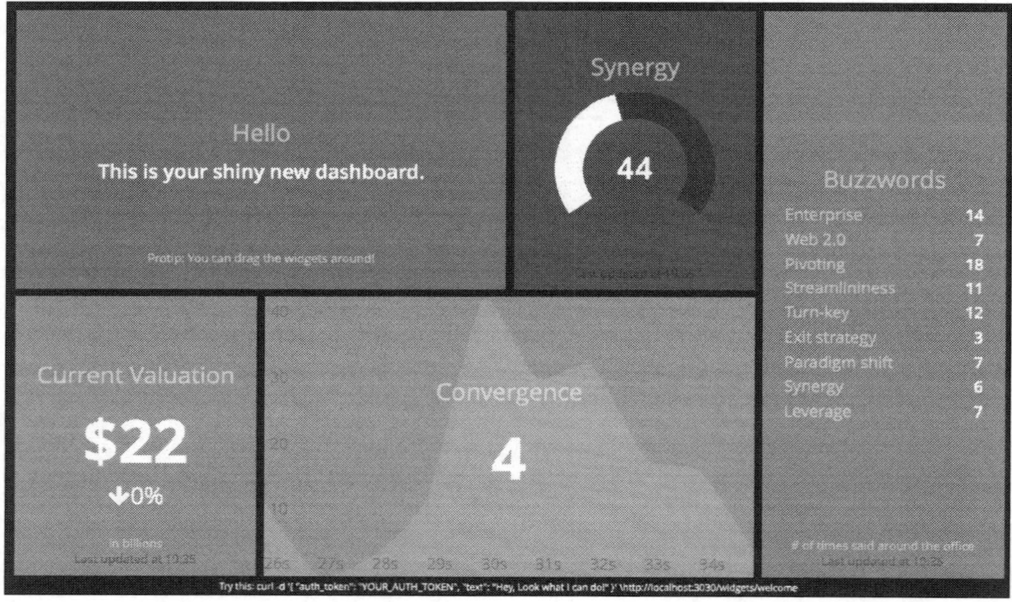

That's looking pretty good, and it proves that your installation is working fine. We're now ready to start creating our own dashboards and populating them with data.

Creating our dashboard

The first step to creating our own dashboard is to create our own layout of widgets to represent our data. We want to ensure that our prospective users have enough data to tell them how Puppet is doing in general, but we also don't want to overload them with data. We're going to introduce the following items onto our dashboard:

- Number of hosts that have changed in the past 30 minutes
- Number of hosts with pending changes in the past 30 minutes

- Number of hosts that failed a resource in the past 30 minutes
- List of nodes that have failed their Puppet run
- Number of hosts Puppet is managing at this point in time
- The total number of managed resources
- The average number of managed resources per node

These details give our users a good amount of information without overloading them with extraneous detail; they should be able to very quickly see if everything is running fine. And if there are issues, such as a large amount of changed or failed hosts, they should be immediately apparent at a glance.

Creating our dashboard layout

Let's go ahead and create our dashboard layout. Navigate to the `dashboards` directory within the `puppetdash` project and create a new file called `puppet.erb`. By default, Dashing will load the example dashboard as its default dashboard, and unless you change the default dashboard, you are going to have to type the path to your dashboard each time. Typing is tedious, and defaults are much more fun; let's go ahead and change the setting to make our new layout the default dashboard. Open the `puppetdash/config.ru` file in your favorite editor and locate the following lines of code within it:

```
configure do
set :auth_token, 'YOUR_AUTH_TOKEN'
```

Now, edit this code so that it looks as follows:

```
configure do
set :auth_token, 'YOUR_AUTH_TOKEN'
set :default_dashboard, 'puppet'
```

Go ahead and start your dashboard using the `dashing start` command. Now, you should find that it loads a blank dashboard on startup, as there is nothing in the `dashboards/puppet.erb` file for it to display. Let's go ahead and amend that; open the `puppet.erb` file in your editor and insert the following code:

```
<% content_for :title do %>Puppet Stats<% end %>
<div class="gridster">
  <ul>
    <li data-row="1" data-col="1" data-sizex="1" data-sizey="1">
      <div data-id="pupchanged" data-view="Number" data-
        title="Changed" style="background-color:#96bf48"></div>
    </li>
```

```
    <li data-row="1" data-col="1" data-sizex="1" data-sizey="1">
      <div data-id="puppending" data-view="Number" data-
        title="Pending" ></div>
    </li>

    <li data-row="1" data-col="1" data-sizex="1" data-sizey="1">
      <div data-id="pupfailed" data-view="Number" data-
        title="Failed" class="status-danger"></div>
    </li>

    <li data-row="1" data-col="1" data-sizex="1" data-sizey="2">
      <div data-id="failedhosts" data-view="Text" data-
        title="Failed Hosts"></div>
    </li>

    <li data-row="1" data-col="1" data-sizex="1" data-sizey="1">
      <div data-id="manhosts" data-view="Number" data-
        title="Managed hosts" style="background-
        color:#737373"></div>
    </li>

    <li data-row="1" data-col="1" data-sizex="1" data-sizey="1">
      <div data-id="manresources" data-view="Number" data-
        title="Managed Resources" style="background-
        color:#737373"></div>
    </li>

    <li data-row="1" data-col="1" data-sizex="1" data-sizey="1">
      <div data-id="avgresources" data-view="Number" data-
        title="Average Resources Per node" style="background-
        color:#737373"></div>
    </li>

  </ul>
</div>
```

This is essentially a simple HTML code that lays out a series of list items within an unordered list. Each of these items represents an individual widget. Let's look in a little more detail at how one of our widgets is defined. Consider the following code snippet:

```
<li data-row="1" data-col="1" data-sizex="1" data-sizey="1">
  <div data-id="pupchanged" data-view="Number" data-
    title="Changed" style="background-color:#96bf48"></div>
</li>
```

Widget definitions are made up of several options. The universally supported options are the following:

- `data-row` and `data-col`: These two tags are used to define the widget's starting position on the grid, and are simply expressed as Cartesian coordinates. Note that this is the starting position; Dashing supports drag and drop rearrangement, so don't be surprised if you wander past the TV you are displaying your dashboard on to find it looks different!
- `data-id`: This tag is used to subscribe a widget to a particular Dashing job; in our case, we're subscribed to the `pupchanged` job. So, every time that job sends updated information, it will be updated in any widget that is subscribed to it via the `data-id` tag. You can have multiple widgets subscribed to the same job, which is excellent for jobs (akin to the PuppetDB scan that we have). You want to keep down the number of times you perform heavy queries to data sources wherever possible.
- `data-view`: This tag defines the type of widget. It may be a number, text, list, and so on. By default, Dashing ships with several different widgets, and you can find these in the `widgets` directory of your Dashing application. The tag needs to match the directory name of your chosen widget in that directory.
- `data-title`: This tag defines the heading that will be shown on the widget and can be a free-form piece of text of your choice.
- Additional tags: As you can see, I've added several additional tags to some of the widgets; this is to style the color of the tiles. Generally speaking, you can use most of the common CSS tags to apply styling to the tiles, but be careful with any tags that affect the positioning or layout, as these can have severely weird effects on the grid.

Go ahead and save this file and then refresh your browser. You should have a dashboard that looks like the following screenshot:

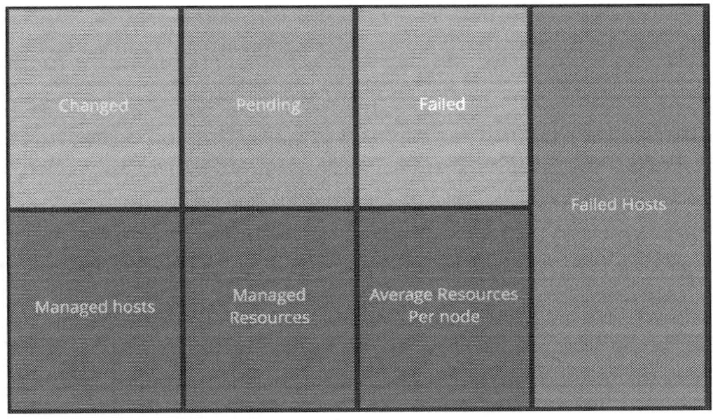

As you can see, the dashboard is using color to great effect to delineate the different data types. Note that in the dashboard, the **Failed** tile is gently pulsating. This is due to the `class="status-danger"` class that we set for this widget within the layout; this causes the tile to gently pulsate and will focus user attention on it. There is also an additional class called `class="status-warning"` that causes the tile to turn a rather alarming shade of red as well as pulsate. This can be used to great effect if you have something you really urgently need a user to notice.

At present, the dashboard looks nice, but it isn't especially useful. Let's go ahead and start creating the jobs that are going to feed data into our dashboard.

Feeding data into Dashing

As we've already covered, Dashing uses a series of scheduled jobs written in Ruby that will collect any data that we are interested in. A library called `rufus-scheduler` controls the scheduling; the `rufus-scheduler` library allows for great flexibility as to when and how jobs are run, meaning that you could have a lightweight job that scrapes data from a public API and runs every five seconds, and another job that will run every 30 minutes and perform a heavy query on a database.

We're going to create a single job called `puppet.rb`, and this Ruby code is going to perform the following actions:

- Gather metrics using PuppetDB's `metrics` endpoint
- Gather a list of nodes using PuppetDB's `nodes` endpoint
- Use the nodes gathered to gather counts for events that have occurred in the past 30 minutes using PuppetDB's `event-counts` endpoint
- Parse the events data to display the state of our hosts

As you can see, we're taking the knowledge that we've gained with PuppetDB over the past two chapters and putting it to good use.

Firstly, let's clear out the jobs that ship with Dashing. These are used to populate the demo dashboards and aren't going to be used by us. However, they will still run. Any Ruby file within the `jobs` directory will be executed, and although it won't affect our dashboard directly, it will output warnings about the Twitter job into the console when you run the dashboard. Let's avoid confusion and save a tiny amount of resources by getting rid of those now by simply deleting every `.rb` file within the `jobs` directory. You can do this by executing the following command in the root of your Dashing project:

```
rm jobs/*.rb
```

Creating new jobs in Dashing

Now that we have a nice and clean `jobs` directory, let's create a new job. We can use a utility built into Dashing to build a skeleton job for us. At the command prompt, change your current directory to the `puppetdash` project root and issue the following command:

```
dashing generate job puppet
```

This will create a new file called `puppet.rb` and place it in the `jobs` directory of our dashboard. Open up the file and take a look. It has the following code:

```
# :first_in sets how long it takes before the job is first run. In
this case, it is run immediately
SCHEDULER.every '1m', :first_in => 0 do |job|
send_event('widget_id', { })
end
```

As you can see, we have the beginnings of our job. The layout is very simple; the first line after the comment sets how often this job will run using the `every` method of the `rufus-scheduler` library. We also ensure that this job will run as soon as we start the dashboard using the `:first_in` option; this is essentially a numerical value in seconds that the scheduler will wait before running the first job. Setting it to zero will ensure that the job runs straight away. This is a useful option if you need to ensure that some of your jobs are staggered to avoid excess load on external systems.

Next, we create a Ruby block called `job` that will contain the actual code that will gather and send data. Essentially, this is a loop with code being executed every *n* units, where *n* could be seconds, minutes, hours, or days, depending on the call to the `SCHEDULER.every` method. As you can see, the default value is every one minute, but by setting the option to `1s`, it would run every second, and setting it to `1h` would ensure it runs every hour. You can find out more about which time formats the `rufus-scheduler` library understands by visiting the project page at `http://rufus.rubyforge.org/rufus-scheduler/`.

Let's go ahead and edit this code to suit our purposes. The first thing we're going to do is include the libraries that we will need to work with our data; these are old friends we've already worked with when using PuppetDB and should be familiar at this point. We're also going to set our job to run every 30 seconds; we're going to be hitting PuppetDB reasonably hard, so we don't want to be too heavy handed, and this type of data doesn't need to be in real time. Have a look at the following code:

```
require 'json'
require 'net/http'
require 'uri'
```

```
# :first_in sets how long it takes before the job is first run. In
  this case, it is run immediately
SCHEDULER.every '30s', :first_in => 0, allow_overlapping: false do
```

It's worth noting the additional option I've added to the scheduler; that is, the `allow_overlapping: false` option. This ensures that this job won't run until all previous iterations of this job have completed. This ensures that if PuppetDB takes longer than 30 seconds to respond, we don't add to its woes by sending yet another set of queries for it to deal with.

Now that we have our job schedule defined, it's time to move on and start gathering data. Firstly, let's define some variables to hold our data. This is described in the following code snippet:

```
SCHEDULER.every '30s',  :first_in => 0, allow_overlapping: false do
|puppet|

time_past = (Time.now - 1800)
ftime_now = Time.now.strftime("%FT%T")
ftime_past = time_past.strftime("%FT%T")

  @failedhosts = []
  @failed = 0
  @changed = 0
  @unchanged = 0
  @pending = 0
  @eventtext = ''
```

What we're doing here is setting up three variables for holding time data. The first variable (`time_past`) holds the current time minus 30 minutes; this gives us the time period we want to report on. The other two time variables (`ftime_now` and `ftime_past`) are formatted ready for submission to PuppetDB. The next six variables are going to be used to hold the data we plan to return, an array of hosts, the number of hosts that Puppet has affected in the past 30 minutes, and finally a place holder to decant our array of hosts into when we come to display it.

Our next task is to fetch the data from PuppetDB using the same methods that we've covered in the previous chapters. This time a round, we're going to be gathering data from a variety of PuppetDB sources, and in particular, we will be using the `metrics` endpoint for the first time. Have a look at the following code:

```
@eventtext = ''

nodes = JSON.parse(Net::HTTP.get_response(URI.parse
  ('http://localhost:8080/v3/nodes/')).body)
```

```
numberofhosts = JSON.parse(Net::HTTP.get_response(URI.parse
  ('http://localhost:8080/v3/metrics/mbean/com.puppetlabs.puppetdb.
  query.population:type=default,name=num-nodes' )).body)["Value"]

numberofresources = JSON.parse(Net::HTTP.get_response(URI.parse
  ('http://localhost:8080/v3/metrics/mbean/com.puppetlabs.puppetdb.
  query.population:type=default,name=num-resources' )).body)["Value"]

avgresources  = JSON.parse(Net::HTTP.get_response(URI.parse
  ('http://localhost:8080/v3/metrics/mbean/com.puppetlabs.puppetdb.
  query.population:type=default,name=avg-resources-per-node'
  )).body)["Value"].round
```

You may be thinking that the call to the `nodes` endpoint looks a little different than before; this is because this time a round, we're performing the JSON parse, the `NET::HTTP` library call, and the URI parse all in one line. This is a more efficient method, but is slightly less readable on first reading; by now, you should be familiar with using this technique—this is just making it tidier.

The `metrics` endpoint is another PuppetDB endpoint that is simple to work with as it is a single non-parameterized call that responds with a single JSON element. As you can see, we're taking the value returned by that call (contained within the `["Value"]` field) and assigning it straight to its respective variable; there's no more processing required for the metrics.

So, we now have our list of nodes and our metrics, and we now need to calculate the data we need to fill our required columns. Take another look at our dashboard:

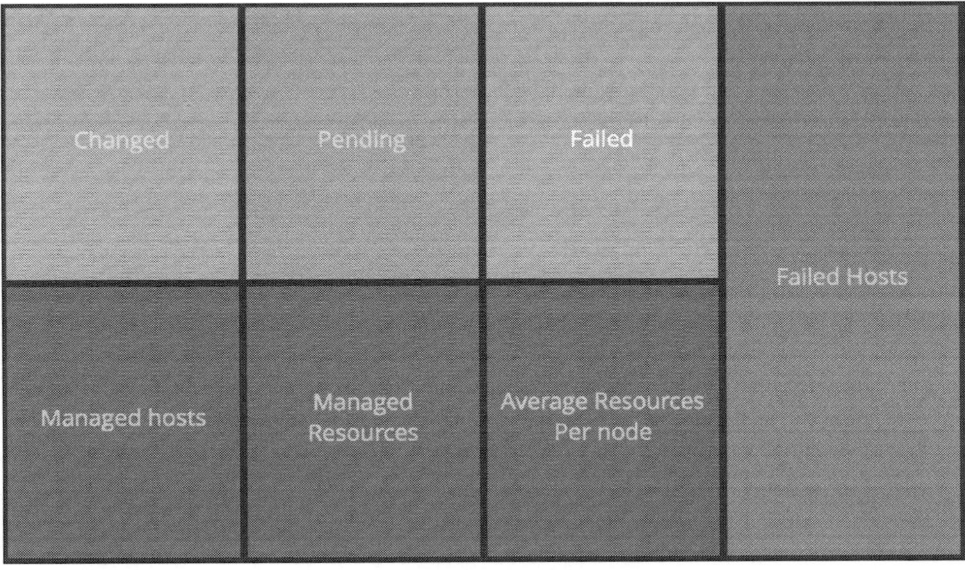

We now need a way to calculate how many hosts are in a particular state. Normally, we would turn to the `aggregate-event-counts` endpoint for this information. As we've noted in earlier chapters, it's a highly efficient endpoint to gather this kind of metric. However, in this case, it doesn't quite fit the bill. The problem with the `aggregate-event-counts` endpoint is that hosts can be counted more than once as it's counting events rather than hosts. Consider this example: a host tries to apply both a user and file resource from its catalog, with the user resource applying OK, but the file resource failing due to a missing prerequisite. In this scenario, the host has created two events, one success and one failure, and this will be reflected in the final events count.

As our dashboard is taking the point of view of a node, it makes more sense to ensure that a host can only be in one of three states: changed, pending, or failed. This maps nicely to the success, noop, and failure event types. We just need to ensure that if a host correctly applies three resources and fails on the fourth, then that is reflected in the **Failed** tile of the dashboard and doesn't appear in the **Changed** tile. Although technically it is both, for our dashboard, we want to ensure that it's only reported as failed. Let's go ahead and add the following code to enable this for the `puppet.rb` file:

```
nodes.each do |node|
  uri = URI.parse('http://localhost:8080/v3/event-counts/')
  uri.query = URI.encode_www_form(:query => %Q'["and", ["=",
"certname", "#{node['name']}"],["<", "timestamp", "#{ftime_
now}"],[">", "timestamp", "#{ftime_past}"],["=", "latest-report?",
"true"]]', :'summarize-by' => 'certname', :'count-by' => 'resource')

  events = JSON.parse(Net::HTTP.get_response(uri).body)
  events.each do |event|
    if event['failures'] > 0
      @failedhosts << event['subject']['title']
      @failed += 1
    elsif event['noops'] > 0
      @pending += 1
    elsif event['successes'] > 0
      @changed += 1
    end

  end
end
```

The first thing that we are doing is constructing a Ruby block and passing it the name of the node we gathered from the nodes list. We then connect to the `event-counts` endpoint and query it for any events created by this node in the past 30 minutes. This is derived by asking for any events that fall between the `ftime_past` (30 minutes ago) and `ftime_now` (current time) values.

Once we have our list of events, we need to decide if they constitute a success, failure, or noop operation; we do this by examining the data contained within the event hash, looking for failures, noops, and successes. These are numeric fields that will simply list the number of resources that are in a given state, and we can use this to build our node metrics. It's important that we parse this data in the correct order, as a node may have several different states. To accomplish this, we first check to see if the node has any failed resources, and if it does, we add its hostname to the array we are going to use to build our list of failed nodes. Then, we increment the failed nodes counter before exiting the loop. If it hasn't failed any resources, we then see if it has any non-applied resources, and if it does, we increment the noop counter and exit. Finally, we check if it has successfully applied resources, and if it has, we increment the success counter. By ensuring that we exit the loop after each state is discovered, we avoid a double or even triple counting of a host.

We've gathered all of the data that we need to send to our dashboard view. Now, all we need to do is go ahead and make our widgets aware that there is new data to display. We do this using the `send_event` method provided by Dashing. The `send_event` method uses two arguments: the first is the ID of the widget to which you want to send the data, and the second is the data that you wish the widget to process in JSON format.

In our case, we have the following data IDs:

- `pupfailed`
- `puppending`
- `pupchanged`
- `manhosts`
- `manresources`
- `avgresources`
- `failedhosts`

Each of these IDs in turn map to a particular widget. This is shown in the following screenshot:

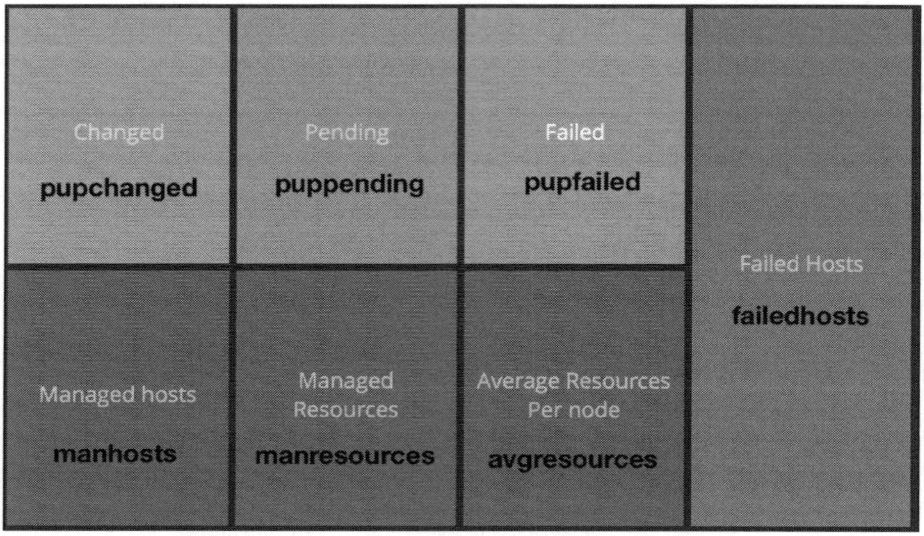

When we trigger a `send_event` method with any of these widget IDs, the displayed data will change to whatever we have sent, assuming that it's in the right format. In our case, we're almost exclusively dealing with data views using the number format; the odd one out is the **Failed** widget, which is using a simple text format.

So, now that we know where the data is going, let's send it. This is done using the following code:

```
send_event('pupfailed', {current: @failed})
send_event('puppending', {current: @pending})
send_event('pupchanged', {current: @changed})
send_event('manhosts', {current: numberofhosts})
send_event('manresources', {current: numberofresources})
send_event('avgresources', {current: avgresources})

  @failedhosts.each do |host|
      @eventtext<< "#{host} \n"
end

send_event('failedhosts', { text: @eventtext })

end
```

This code is fairly straightforward. The first six lines simply take the numeric values we've gathered for our various host metrics and send them on to their respective widgets. As you can see, we are only including one JSON field with each of these, which is the `current:` field. This sets the value of the data that is displayed to the user.

The next set of lines deals with the failed hosts' data. We're sending that to a text widget, so we need to take the data that is currently in an array and iterate through it, adding each line into a variable that we're going to use to hold it as a string object. Note that within each iteration, we're adding the control character `\n` at the end. This is so that each host is followed by a carriage return to ensure our list is nice and tidy.

That's it! You should now be able to go into the root of your Dashing project and run it using the command `dashing start`. You should then see your own version of the dashboard that looks like the following screenshot:

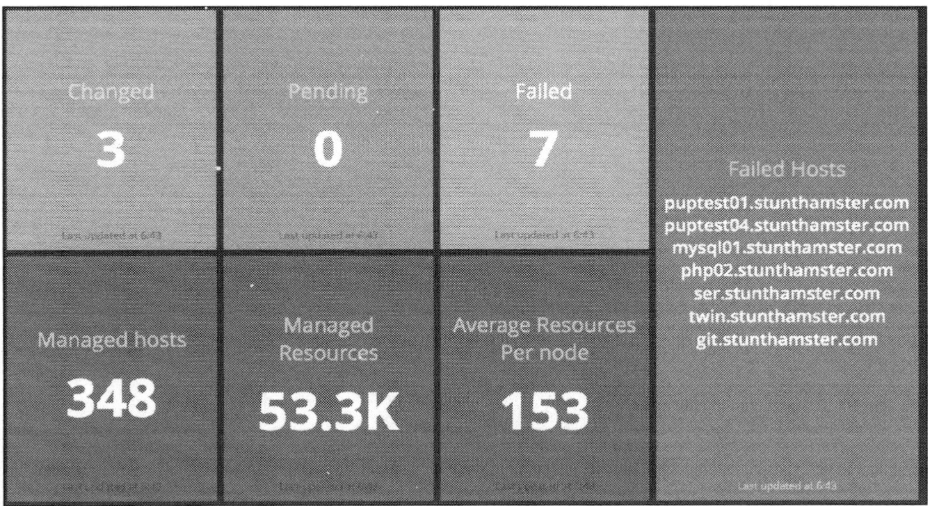

That's a pretty good-looking dashboard, and it makes your most important Puppet metrics both highly accessible and also very clear and easy to read. Dashing has been designed to be displayed on big displays, so if you have a spare TV or a large monitor sitting around the office, it's worth putting this dashboard somewhere nice and visible. As I've mentioned elsewhere, Puppet reporting is a great place to spot when things have radically changed on your network, so having this data at hand can ensure that you see issues before they become big problems.

Adding trends

Our dashboard is already looking pretty good, but Dashing offers a few features that are both easy to implement and quickly and easily add additional data and means of discovery. One of the quickest and easiest additions is adding trends to our Puppet metrics to allow people to see at a glance how data is changing over time. This is achieved using the numbers widget that we've already used. The numbers widget is not just limited to displaying the current dataset; it can also display a second field, which is the percentage change from the last run, complete with an appropriate arrow to denote how the data has changed.

As we've already mentioned, the numbers widget accepts fields in JSON format; we've already given it one field, `:current`, and now we're going to give it a second field, `:last`. This will give the numbers widget the data it needs to draw the trend data, and this `:last` field represents the last reading that this widget displayed. Let's go ahead and alter our code to add this new feature.

In essence, all we need to do is create three new variables, and these will be used to contain the previous values of the metrics widgets. This is very easy. One of the advantages of using the `rufus-scheduler` library is that the job is effectively running in its own thread. This means that any variables that are initialized can be treated as being persistent for the lifetime of the dashboard process.

Take a look at the following example code for a dashboard job:

```
foo = 0

SCHEDULER.every '5s,' do  |example|

lastfoo = foo
foo += 1

send_event('foo', {current: foo, last: lastfoo })
end
```

In this case, in its first run, the widget will receive two values: the `current:` field value, which will be `1`, and the `last:` field value, which will be `0`. In the next run, the values will be `2` and `1`, then `3` and `2`, and so on. Essentially, the code between the `SCHEDULER.every` method and the `end` statement is being continuously run, and thus the values are being persisted. This is helpful as it saves you using something along the lines of a text file, database, or key value store to store this data, and avoids the overhead of having to retrieve it every time you want to refresh your dataset. Dashing also keeps a history of the widget values, which means that when you restart the dashboard, it should load the previous values and avoid you having to start from scratch. You can find this in the root of your `dashing` folder in a file named `history.yaml`.

Let's go ahead and edit our code to support the trends view. First of all, we need to create some blank variables to hold our data. This is described in the following code:

```
require 'json'
require 'net/http'
require 'uri'

last_manhosts = 0
last_manresources = 0
last_avgresources = 0
```

Now, we need to assign them a value within the actual job loop itself. This is described in the following code snippet:

```
time_past = (Time.now - 1800)
ftime_now = Time.now.strftime("%FT%T")
ftime_past = time_past.strftime("%FT%T")

last_manhosts = numberofhosts
last_manresources = numberofresources
last_avgresources = avgresources
```

This code is applied before any other calculation, and so should either contain `0` if this is the very first time the dashboard has run, or the previous value of the `manhosts`, `manresources`, and `avgresources` IDs if it has been run before. Finally, we need to send our data to the widget. This is done using the following code:

```
send_event('pupfailed', {current: @failed})
send_event('puppending', {current: @pending})
send_event('pupchanged', {current: @changed})
send_event('manhosts', {current: numberofhosts,
  last:last_manhosts})
send_event('manresources', {current: numberofresources,
  last:last_manresources})
send_event('avgresources', {current: avgresources,
  last:last_avgresources})
```

That's all we need to do. None of the layout information has changed, and the number widget is already designed to deal with our new data. Go ahead and restart your dashboard. It should now look like the following screenshot:

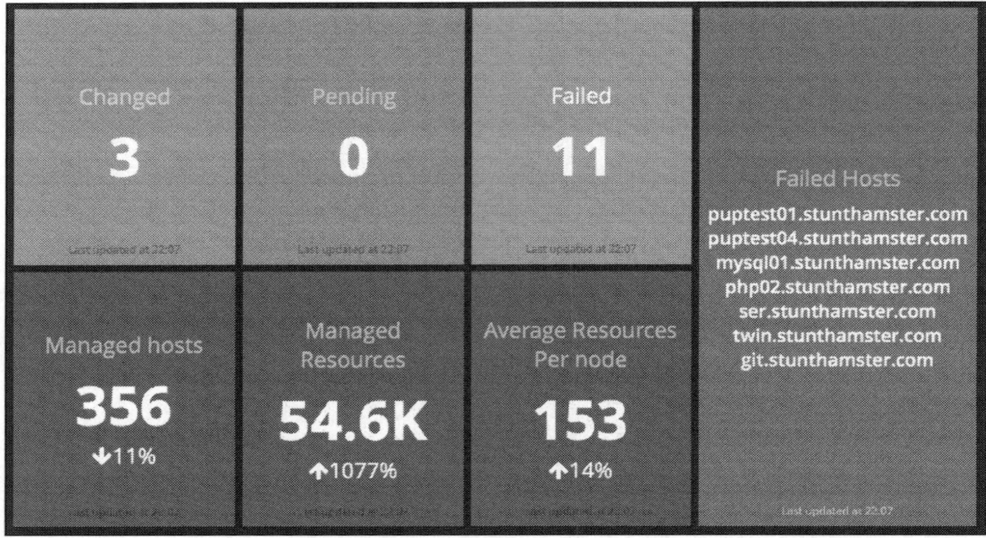

As you can see, we can now easily see the trends by simply glancing at the panel. In this example, my managed resources have gone through the roof and my average resources per node are way up. But my managed hosts have dropped alarmingly. If this were a production system, I'd be reaching for the panic button around this point. Without the dashboard, I might have been blissfully unaware of any problems until it moved from being a curious problem to becoming a huge, stability threatening monstrosity of an incident. Much like riding a bike on the road, when it comes to infrastructure management, visibility is your friend.

Adding meters

We've made our trends easier to see, but the dashboard still lacks a certain flair. Sure it's clear and very colorful, but it's still pretty static. Let's make it a bit swishier and add some swing to our dashboard using the meter widget. The meter widget is a fun way of not only adding some animation to a dashboard, but also giving users a visual clue as to how dramatically things have changed.

Firstly, let's amend our `puppet.erb` file. As we covered earlier, the `.erb` file deals with the layout for the dashboard, and in particular, it is where you define the types of widgets that will be presented. In our case, we want to take the existing number widgets and turn them into meter widgets. You can do this by amending the `puppet.erb` file to contain the following code snippet:

```
<% content_for :title do %>Puppet Stats<% end %>
<div class="gridster">
<ul>


<li data-row="1" data-col="1" data-sizex="1" data-sizey="1">
  <div data-id="pupchanged" data-view="Meter" data-min=
    "0 data-max="100" style="background-color:#96bf48"></div>
</li>


<li data-row="1" data-col="1" data-sizex="1" data-sizey="1">
  <div data-id="puppending" data-view="Meter" data-min=
    "0" data-max="100" ></div>
</li>

<li data-row="1" data-col="1" data-sizex="1" data-sizey="1">
  <div data-id="pupfailed" data-view="Meter" data-min=
    "0" data-max="100" class="status-danger"></div>
</li>
```

As you can see, we've slightly amended the HTML code to include a new `data-view` attribute, and we've added some additional attributes to control the minimum and maximum numbers. Go ahead and change these attributes to reflect your environment. Generally speaking, I'd make the `data-max` value match the number of hosts. This controls the distance that the meter can swing, so you want the top end to be roughly analogous to the number of hosts you have.

The next thing we need to do is edit our job code. Although the widget ID remains the same, the widget type is different, and will therefore accept a slightly different format of data. Go ahead and amend your code to look like the following:

```
send_event('pupfailed', {value: @failed})
send_event('puppending', {value: @pending})
send_event('pupchanged', {value: @changed})
send_event('manhosts', {current: numberofhosts,
  last:last_manhosts})
```

```
send_event('manresources', {current: numberofresources,
  last:last_manresources})
send_event('avgresources', {current: avgresources,
  last:last_avgresources})
```

As you can see, all we've done is changed the format of the data from the `current:` type to the `value:` type. The rest remains the same as the meter widget deals in numeric data in the same way as the number widget. OK, now that we've made our changes, go ahead and restart our Dashing dashboard. You should end up with a dashboard that looks like the following screenshot:

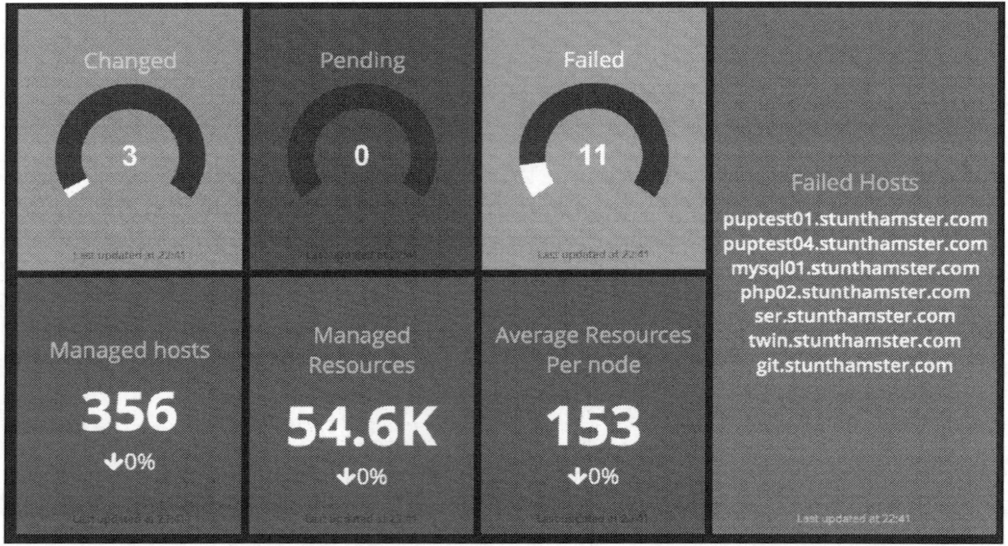

Now we have a dashboard that is gaudily colorful, nicely informative, and rather impressively animated. This is now ready to be put up on the largest monitor or TV you have to hand so that you can keep an eye on it.

As you can see, Dashing is a versatile accompaniment to PuppetDB. Hopefully, this simple dashboard has set your imagination to work wondering what else you could display. Remember, PuppetDB has access not only to the Puppet catalog and reports, but also the Facter information for each host. This can make for a fairly impressive range of data. Want to easily graph how many CPUs you currently have allocated? Ever wondered how much RAM your hosts in a certain domain have? All these facts and more are relatively easy to retrieve using PuppetDB and very easy to display using Dashing. I encourage you to play around and see what combinations you can come up with. Also, remember that you're not just limited to one dashboard using Dashing – you can create as many as you like within the `dashboards` folder.

As long as there is a job that can feed your widgets with data, it doesn't matter how many you have. If you are going to employ a large amount of dashboards, then it might be sensible to use a generic Puppet job to retrieve the data. That way, you have a singular job that runs every so often and gathers all of the stats from PuppetDB and feeds many dashboards, rather than having many dashboards, each with their own individual jobs to gather data. This is the kind of shenanigans that can leave your PuppetDB a smoking ruin by subjecting it to a very large load every few seconds as your many widgets go looking for their data.

Summary

In this chapter, we've taken a look at how we can utilize the data we store in PuppetDB to create attractive dashboards in Dashing. We've explored the use of ERB templates to lay out our widgets and the concept of using jobs to gather data in the background. We've created our own dashboards to allow our users to see the current state of the Puppet infrastructure, including which resources have changed, succeeded, and failed. We've taken that basic dashboard and improved it by adding in a quick and easy trends reference, and we also added some more graphical cues by adding in meters to accentuate some of the data display. Finally, we took a look at some general tips on how to get the best out of your dashboard data.

In the next chapter, we're going to take a look back at everything we've covered so far and recap some of the highlights. We're also going to explore some of the other ways you can use your Puppet data, and briefly touch on what other tools you can use to drive reporting and alerting using Puppet.

9 Looking Back and Looking Forward

We are nearing the end of our exploration of Puppet reporting and alerting, and so it seems fitting that we spend this chapter going over what we've learned and exploring some of the other ways in which you can utilize the reporting functions of Puppet.

In this chapter, we will cover:

- A recap of Puppet dashboards and integration with third-party dashboards
- Looking back at the alerting feature and integration with external alerting systems
- Analyzing metrics and changes with **Graphite**
- Anomaly detection with **Etsy Skyline**
- Driving change and orchestration with the Puppet reporting feature

Looking back at what we've learned

By now, you should be familiar with Puppet reporting features and how they fit in with the wider Puppet product. However, it's worth recapping what we've learned, and while we recap, we will look at other ways of using these features. We've covered the basics of configuration and data retrieval in this book, but this is just the tip of the iceberg. With a little imagination and creative use of both the report processors and PuppetDB features, you can start to use Puppet in ways you may not have considered, not only to uncover details about your infrastructure you may not have been aware of, but also to drive change within it.

Rediscovering dashboards

We took a look at dashboards way back in *Chapter 2, Viewing Data in Dashboards*, and you will remember from that chapter that there are several dashboards available for Puppet, ranging from the venerable Puppet Dashboard through to the all singing and all dancing Puppet Enterprise Console. With the addition of PuppetBoard, we also have a stylish and easy to use way to observe the details that PuppetDB holds.

Dashboards are a fantastic addition to your Puppet infrastructure, allowing you to see, at a glance, any element of your infrastructure that is either not configured correctly or, perhaps more importantly, has recently been updated. The visibility of changes is perhaps one of the most bewilderingly overlooked and yet impressive features that Puppet offers, and the dashboard is your window into that process.

In *Chapter 8, Creating Your Own Custom Dashboard*, we looked at how we can use Puppet to design our own custom reporting dashboard. This utilized the power of PuppetDB and the simplicity of Dashing to create our very own view of Puppet data. We can use the same techniques to add data to other dashboards and aggregation systems. The recent explosion of tools for DevOps system administrators has gifted us with several different cloud-based dashboard systems such as Boundary (`http://boundary.com`) and New Relic (`http://newrelic.com`). These systems are increasingly attempting to become the hub of a busy DevOps department and offer some excellent integration, both for data visualization and alerting. Using custom report processors, Puppet can easily be integrated into these systems and will bring valuable insight into the rate of change alongside the other metrics that these applications monitor. We have long become accustomed to the idea that we need to track changes to our application code; however, for some time, we have lacked the tools to do this with our infrastructure. Using Puppet reporting, we can start to bridge that gap, and by integrating with existing dashboards used to visualize this data, we can get a holistic view of our rate of change.

Producing alerts

In *Chapter 4, Creating Your Own Report Processor*, we looked at how you can create your own alerts using custom report processors. We used a relatively small amount of Ruby code to monitor change among specific elements, and triggered e-mails when this occurred. This was the basis of our simple and effective alerting system, and for small installations, it would be absolutely perfect. For larger infrastructures, you will need something a little more industrial, with a solution that can both scale and offer a more complete set of features about how you are alerted. Infrastructure monitoring has been around for some considerable time, and there are a great deal of tools to choose from, both open source and commercial.

The recent trend towards having a more ephemeral infrastructure has started to create a shift in this space, with an increasing number of monitoring system developers trying to make their respective systems suitable for use in an environment where server lifetimes may only be measured in hours rather than the more traditional years. Puppet is already being widely utilized to configure these tools as the exported configuration feature makes it incredibly simple to roll out new checks when systems change; in particular, this has made managing the complexities of products based around **Nagios** much simpler.

Using Nagios

Nagios (`http://www.nagios.org`) is the old faithful of the monitoring world, and it's hard to find a systems administrator who hasn't had to work with it at some point in his or her career. This open source project has had the benefit of a huge community of software engineers working on it for quite a number of years, and at this point, could be considered the quintessential open source monitoring tool.

Nagios has been the basis for a great number of new projects, both commercial and open source, with several of them being direct forks from the original Nagios code base.

Discovering Icinga and Shinken

Products such as **Icinga** (`https://www.icinga.org`) and **Shinken** (`http://www.shinken-monitoring.org`) are forked from the Nagios code base, and have taken certain features of the original product and improved upon them for certain use cases. The omnipresence of Nagios has also ensured that most monitoring systems can make use of the incredible number of checks that have been written for it, and will, at the very least, be able to react to output from them.

One very interesting relative newcomer in the monitoring space is the **Sensu** project (`http://sensuapp.org`). Its dashboard is shown in the following screenshot:

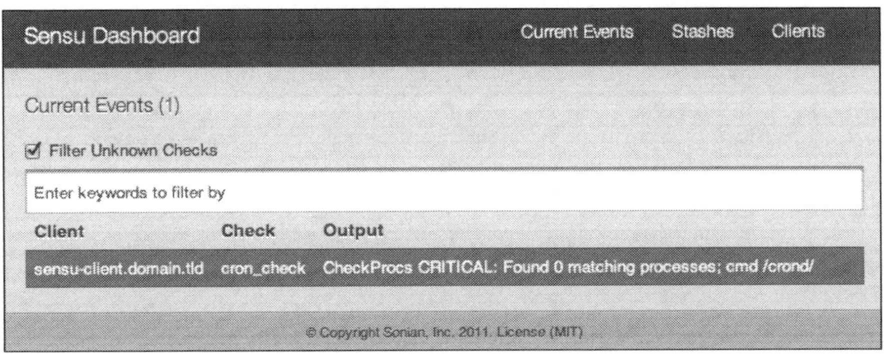

Sensu has been designed from the ground up to be used in large and volatile environments (such as a cloud) and brings design patterns such as a publish and subscribe model, both to enable it to scale to thousands of clients relatively easily and to make the discovery and configuration of new hosts simple. Sensu has been designed with a robust API and the Ruby library to allow the addition of new checks, and although a great many of them are written in Ruby, you can also implement them in pretty much any other language. I've seen checks that have been written in Ruby, Python, and Java. If for some reason, you can't write a new check, Sensu is able to understand and process checks that have been designed for Nagios, so you can easily reuse existing checks.

As we've already discovered, Puppet isn't just limited to setting up these systems. It can also be used to trigger alerts based on its unique view of your infrastructure. This is where it integrates well with a dedicated monitoring system such as Nagios and Sensu. Raising alerts using report processors is relatively easy; however, generating the correct notification type is complex and better left to systems more suited for that activity. Using the techniques we have already learned, it would be easy to add checks like the following:

- Monitor and alert if a resource failed to apply or a catalog failed to compile
- Alert if Puppet has not been run on a host for a certain amount of time
- Alert if certain non-managed resources are changed using the `audit` metaparameter
- Monitor and alert if certain facts have changed on a node using the PuppetDB records

Compliance monitoring with Puppet

In combination with Facter, Puppet knows a huge amount about your infrastructure, and informs your dedicated monitoring system when these facts have changed. By using these facts alongside defined roles within your ENC or Hiera, it's possible to raise alerts when nodes fall out of compliance. With judicious use of custom facts, you can use Puppet to gather details of what software and configuration exists on a given set of servers, store them in PuppetDB, and then use your alerting system to compare those details and set off appropriate warnings if they don't match. By using Puppet to alert you when a host is out of compliance, you gain the confidence that your infrastructure is configured how it needs to be for your uses. Remember, Puppet has the under-utilized `audit` metaparameter, and this is an excellent way to identify and monitor resources that you might not want to manage using Puppet. We looked at how to use the `audit` metaparameter in *Chapter 4, Creating Your Own Report Processor*; it's worth learning this technique as it can add simple, powerful, and real-time auditing to your Puppet-managed infrastructure.

Auditing isn't limited to the elements that Puppet manages, as you can easily create custom facts whose only role is to gather data for consumption by your reporting and alerting systems. Creative use of custom facts can be hugely beneficial when tying your alerting systems with Puppet; it's relatively easy to write a custom fact to export all the installed software on a given server or to return details about custom systems designed by your internal developers. Once these facts have been created, they are available for use in report processors and are also stored in PuppetDB for reporting uses. Be creative - the more monitoring you have, the more you can be confident that your systems are correctly configured, ready for use, and suited for the applications that are going to be hosted on them. There is nothing more irritating than being woken up at some unnatural time of the morning by a customer who has spotted a problem because your alerting system missed it.

Analyzing metrics with StatsD, Graphite, and Etsy Skyline

As we have seen throughout this book, Puppet creates an awful lot of interesting metrics, with items such as total number of managed resources, time taken to apply catalog, and so on readily available to report against. On its own, this can be of limited use - you can certainly raise alerts based around long-running clients, and the stats for the number of managed hosts and resources can be a handy gauge of activity, but in general, these stats are more suited to analysis rather than alerting. Luckily, we now have some very powerful tools at our disposal to not only store this type of data, but also to analyze and visualize it.

Graphite (`https://github.com/graphite-project`) is one such system, and is a popular and highly powerful system for storing and graphing time series data.

> A time series is essentially points of data plotted over a set time period. For instance, the response time of an application measured at intervals of a minute would be an excellent example.

This is a perfect fit for Puppet metrics, and getting Puppet metrics into Graphite is very easy indeed. You can find a ready-made report processor at `https://github.com/krux/puppet-module-graphite-report`, which once installed will send your Puppet metrics to Graphite.

Graphite allows you to start graphing your Puppet metrics in real time and easily combine disparate data points into a single graph. For instance, in Puppet metrics terms, this means that you could take the metrics for the catalog compilation time and overlay them with the number of resources managed. This is pretty interesting stuff, but it's when you combine this with other data sources that things can become really interesting. By installing collectd (`http://collectd.org`) onto your Puppet master, you can start to gather CPU and memory usage statistics as well as disk I/O and other important system performance data points. collectd can send this data into Graphite, and once in there, you can easily create real-time graphs that overlay your detailed Puppet metrics against the amount of resources that are being consumed. This allows you to very easily create scalability reports for your Puppet infrastructure and determine when you might need to consider scaling up your systems.

Tracking changes with Puppet and Graphite

You can also start to use your Puppet data in a more holistic way. One of the metrics that people overlook when they are looking at their infrastructure is the rate of change. For instance, you may have huge amounts of reporting around requests per second, response time, and resource usage. This is certainly interesting and valuable, but a surprising amount of people miss the simple metrics that tie it all together: deployments and changes. Using Graphite, it would be perfectly simple to create a new index to track Puppet change events, and you could then use a simple Puppet report processor to output a change event every time a host reports that a resource has changed during the course of a Puppet run. This is incredibly useful as it means that you can tie this information into other statistics that you track. For instance, if you notice that your response time on an important application has started to drop, you can easily see if there were Puppet changes applied around that time, and if there were, you can then easily query your PuppetDB catalog to find out which resources were changed in that time frame. Likewise, you can start to monitor the overall health of your infrastructure, such as CPU and RAM usage, against the amount of change going through. If you also use Puppet to deploy new versions of applications, this too can be tracked as a specific changed event.

Using Etsy Skyline to find your normal

Humans are fantastic at spotting patterns in data, and using a tool such as Graphite in combination with Puppet allows you to easily output huge amounts of data for analyses. However, you have to be looking at the appropriate sets of data to see the pattern, and the double-edged sword of using Puppet to increase your level of information is that there is now more information to try and spot patterns within. Fortunately, there are an increasing number of tools that will sift through this data for you and let you know when something is outside of what it has learned to be normal. One excellent and open source example of these tools is Etsy Skyline. This tool can be seen in the following screenshot:

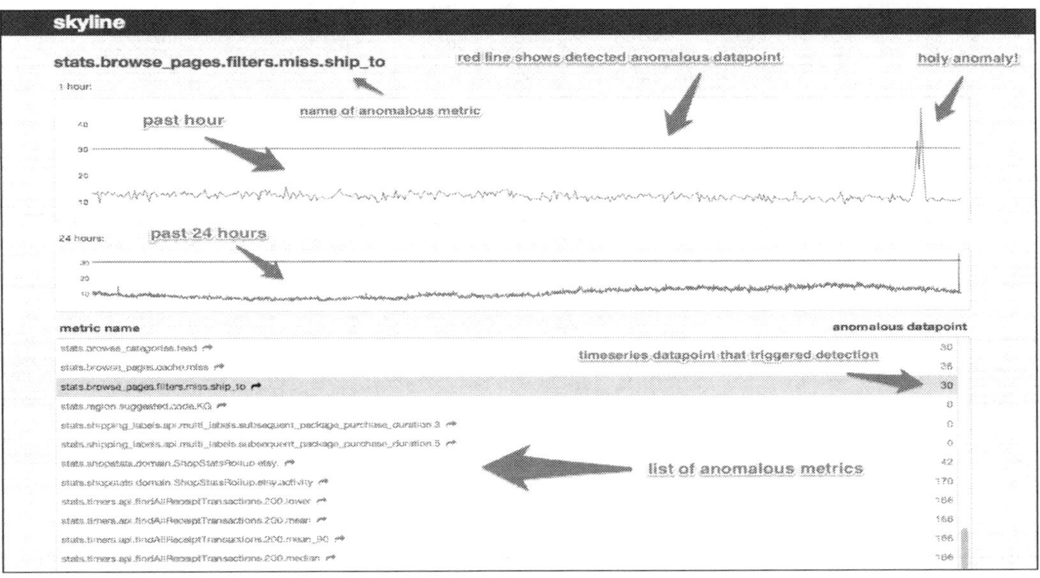

Skyline is able to use Graphite as its data source, and so will start to analyze any and all of the metrics within. Skyline starts to build up a picture of what is considered normal for each of these metrics, and unlike an alerting system such as Nagios, it does not rely on a fixed threshold to decide to alert. For instance, you may find that the CPU of your database host runs at 100 percent every day from 04:00 to 05:00 hours, but is otherwise under 50 percent utilization; this is probably because you are doing housekeeping around that time. Etsy Skyline will soon learn that this is considered normal for your database node and will not do anything when it sees this data; however, if it sees that CPU utilization is at 100 percent in the middle of the day when it hasn't been previously, it will raise an alert and send a snapshot of the data to its web console.

This is incredibly powerful as it allows your tools to crawl through your vast amounts of data and figure out what should be alerted on. It's not a replacement for Nagios or Sensu, but is an incredibly powerful addition to them, and the data that Puppet can provide is a natural fit for this kind of learning system. Over time, you will find that your Puppet changes will start to fall into a natural pattern, especially if you release at predictable times. By adding your Puppet metrics into Graphite and then enabling Etsy Skyline, you will be automatically alerted if some of those metrics start to look a little odd. For instance, you may not be immediately aware if something has caused a huge amount of your Puppet nodes to apply a change, or if your Puppet catalogs are suddenly taking an age to apply. Skyline can be configured to immediately alert you if it sees that something is amiss.

Using Puppet to drive orchestration

Puppet is in the unique position of knowing both when and how something has changed. This is a unique view that allows you to be very creative with orchestrating activity in your network, using Puppet not only to change resources on a given node, but also to then trigger an action that will affect other resources.

A good example would be if you had an application that provided data that other nodes relied on. Now, let's assume that you were forced to push a change to this application that would require the dependent applications to be restarted before they can use the new version. This is something that a Puppet report processor could trigger in conjunction with a suitable orchestration system. In this case, you could use a report processor to monitor a tagged resource (our data providing application), and in the event of that resource being changed, the report processor could send a message to the orchestration system, asking it to perform restarts on the dependent applications. What's neat about this is that you are using Puppet to allow individual resources to communicate with their dependencies and vice versa without needing to bake it into the orchestration layer itself. Another advantage of having Puppet notify the orchestration system is that Puppet knows when a change has been successfully applied; an orchestration system would need to be told what constitutes success. This technique also ensures that it is much harder to miss dependent systems when creating your orchestration steps, as you have started to build an awareness of dependencies within Puppet. Puppet implements the change to an individual resource and then notifies the orchestration system that it needs to carry out an action on the dependencies.

This would be relatively straightforward to implement and would tie in nicely with the Puppet-curated MCollective project (`http://puppetlabs.com/mcollective`). By using Puppet report processors to trigger subsequent actions, you are starting to overcome Puppet's nodal view of the world, and allowing changes to deal with dependencies without manual interaction.

Summary

In this final chapter, we've taken a look at some of the ways you can utilize Puppet reporting and alerting to enhance your understanding of both what is going on within your Puppet infrastructure and also how to leverage the data to create simple yet effective additions to your existing monitoring systems. We've seen how Puppet data can be visualized using either existing dashboards or by creating new ones, and how report processors can be used to drive detailed alerts using existing alerting tools such as Nagios or Sensu. We've also learned about the integration of Puppet with tools such as Graphite, which allow you to utilize Puppet data to both analyze performance and track changes to the infrastructure. We have explored how systems such as Etsy Skyline can be used to learn what is normal within your Puppet infrastructure and set to alert when anomalies occur. We realized how Puppet can be an integral part of orchestration and can trigger actions based on changes to resources.

Now it's over to you; this book has shown you the basics of the Puppet reporting systems and how easy it is to take the data that Puppet creates to drive other activities, be it reporting, alerting, or even orchestration. Hopefully, by now you are looking at the Puppet reporting tools as a gateway that allows Puppet to communicate with the wealth of systems that you are already using to both monitor and report with, and thinking of new ways to use these tools with the additional data that Puppet provides. Puppet reporting brings a huge new set of capabilities, as, traditionally, knowing how and when changes have occurred within your infrastructure has been difficult. Puppet is now making it simple.

I hope that this book has inspired you to create new and interesting applications based around Puppet reporting, and I look forward to seeing the fantastic and novel ways that you put these techniques to use. I truly hope that you share your contributions on GitHub and PuppetForge so that the whole Puppet community can make use of your code. The Puppet reporting features are incredibly powerful, and you're going to have a lot of fun playing with them.

Index

Symbols

A

B

C

P

Thank you for buying
Puppet Reporting and Monitoring

About Packt Publishing

Packt, pronounced 'packed', published its first book "*Mastering phpMyAdmin for Effective MySQL Management*" in April 2004 and subsequently continued to specialize in publishing highly focused books on specific technologies and solutions.

Our books and publications share the experiences of your fellow IT professionals in adapting and customizing today's systems, applications, and frameworks. Our solution based books give you the knowledge and power to customize the software and technologies you're using to get the job done. Packt books are more specific and less general than the IT books you have seen in the past. Our unique business model allows us to bring you more focused information, giving you more of what you need to know, and less of what you don't.

Packt is a modern, yet unique publishing company, which focuses on producing quality, cutting-edge books for communities of developers, administrators, and newbies alike. For more information, please visit our website: `www.packtpub.com`.

About Packt Open Source

In 2010, Packt launched two new brands, Packt Open Source and Packt Enterprise, in order to continue its focus on specialization. This book is part of the Packt Open Source brand, home to books published on software built around Open Source licenses, and offering information to anybody from advanced developers to budding web designers. The Open Source brand also runs Packt's Open Source Royalty Scheme, by which Packt gives a royalty to each Open Source project about whose software a book is sold.

Writing for Packt

We welcome all inquiries from people who are interested in authoring. Book proposals should be sent to `author@packtpub.com`. If your book idea is still at an early stage and you would like to discuss it first before writing a formal book proposal, contact us; one of our commissioning editors will get in touch with you.

We're not just looking for published authors; if you have strong technical skills but no writing experience, our experienced editors can help you develop a writing career, or simply get some additional reward for your expertise.

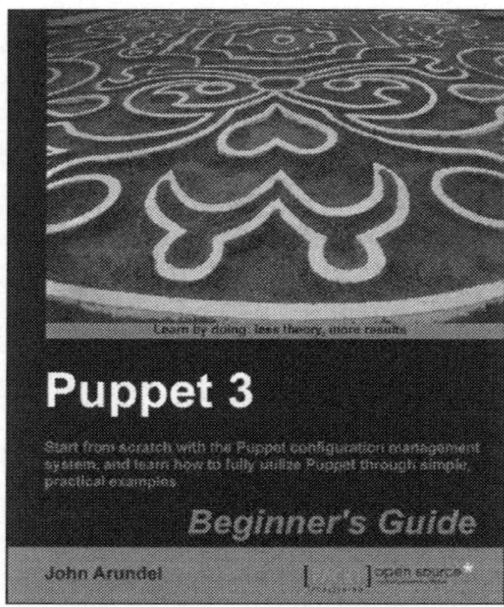

Puppet 3 Beginner's Guide

ISBN: 978-1-78216-124-0 Paperback: 204 pages

Start from scratch with the Puppet configuration management system, and learn how to fully utilize Puppet through simple, practical examples

1. Shows you step-by-step how to install Puppet and start managing your systems with simple examples.

2. Every aspect of Puppet is explained in detail so that you really understand what you're doing.

3. Gets you up and running immediately, from installation to using Puppet for practical tasks in a matter of minutes.

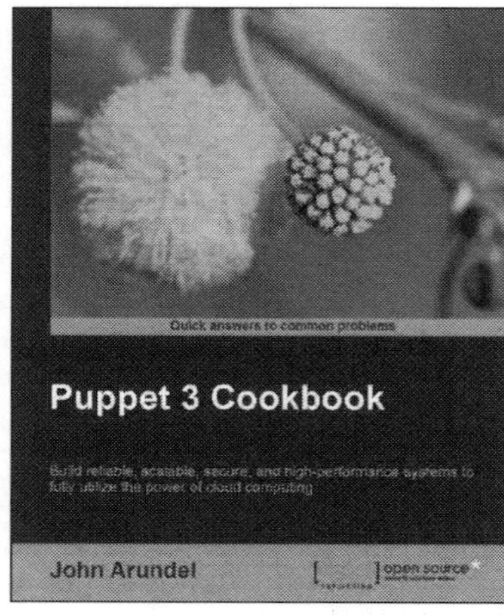

Puppet 3 Cookbook

ISBN: 978-1-78216-976-5 Paperback: 274 pages

Build reliable, scalable, secure, and high-performance systems to fully utilize the power of cloud computing

1. Use Puppet 3 to take control of your servers and desktops, with detailed step-by-step instructions.

2. Covers all the popular tools and frameworks used with Puppet: Dashboard, Foreman, and more.

3. Teaches you how to extend Puppet with custom functions, types, and providers.

Please check **www.PacktPub.com** for information on our titles

Instant Puppet 3 Starter

ISBN: 978-1-78216-174-5 Paperback: 50 pages

Gain complete consistency from your systems with minimal effort using Instant Puppet 3 Starter

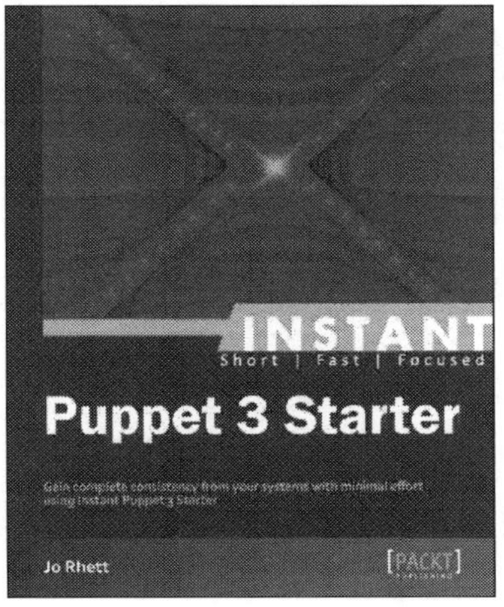

1. Learn something new in an Instant! A short, fast, focused guide delivering immediate results.
2. Learn how deterministic results can vastly reduce your workload.
3. Deploy Puppet Server as a Ruby-on-Rails application to handle thousands of clients.
4. Design your own module for complex configurations.

Chef Infrastructure Automation Cookbook

ISBN: 978-1-84951-922-9 Paperback: 276 pages

Over 80 delicious recipes to automate your cloud and server infrastructure with Chef

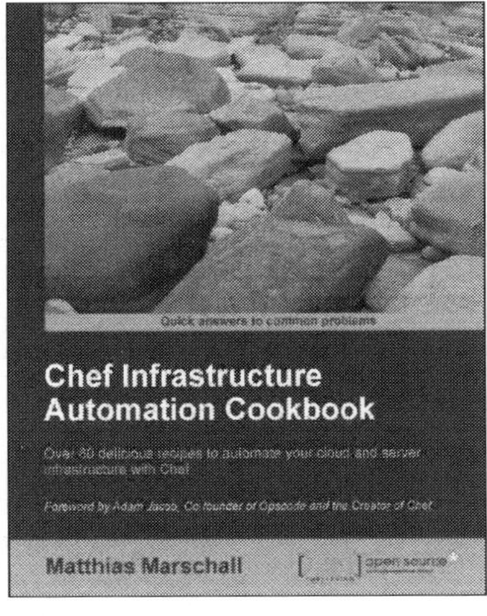

1. Configure, deploy, and scale your applications.
2. Automate error prone and tedious manual tasks.
3. Manage your servers on-site or in the cloud.
4. Solve real world automation challenges with task-based recipes.

Please check **www.PacktPub.com** for information on our titles

Made in the USA
Lexington, KY
04 September 2015